LOOKING OUT FOR NUMBER One

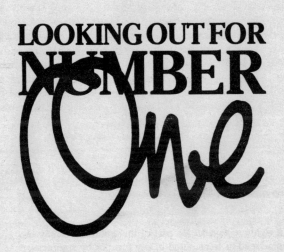

SEMENKO/TUCKER

General
PAPERBACKS

Published in 1990 by
General Paperbacks
34 Lesmill Road
Toronto, Canada
M3B 2T6

First published in hardcover in 1989 by
Stoddart Publishing Co. Limited

ISBN 0-7736-7282-6

Printed and bound in the United States

Contents

FOREWORD

There weren't many goals that I scored as an Edmonton Oiler between 1979 and 1986 that Dave Semenko didn't assist on. Oh, the National Hockey League's record book might not show Dave with that many assists, but believe me, he deserved them.

To score in the NHL, you need first to get into position, then you need time to shoot the puck. During our years with Dave Semenko as a teammate on the Edmonton Oilers, both Jari Kurri and I had lots of time to shoot the puck! In fact Dave made sure that we could shoot the puck from the Players Entrance of every building in the League.

Everyone knows that hockey is a tough sport. With the exception of one or two of us, it's played by very tough guys. Believe me when I say that Dave Semenko was the toughest of the tough. Maybe ever. His reputation for toughness was legendary among the pros — and that was while he was still in junior hockey!

It wasn't by accident that Dave Semenko was one of the most popular Oilers, both with the fans and his teammates. Unless you knew him well, he was a man of few words. He simply played the game to the best of his ability, night in, night out. His style wasn't glamorous, but his effectiveness was measured in Stanley Cup Championship rings.

I'm convinced that Dave Semenko's presence as an Oiler was felt by visiting teams from the moment they started the forty-five minute airport drive into Edmonton. He may be the only player who intimidated opponents into actually not dressing for games!

But what made Dave so special to the fans and his teammates wasn't his toughness, but his ability to keep things in perspective. To remind us all that hockey is only a game. To let us laugh at, and with, one another.

It never bothered Dave that the offensive stars got the recognition. He was just happy to contribute in his own way, to be one of the guys.

When I think of Dave Semenko now, and I often do, I don't picture the piercing glare that caused other heavyweights to look down or up or anywhere but back at David. I remember instead the little smile, the quick wink, and the words "Don't worry, Gretz."

And you know what? I never did.

Wayne Gretzky

1

An Oiler Till I Die

Our plane was about fifteen minutes out of Edmonton when my world stopped. No, we didn't crash. For me, it was much worse than that.

I was in the back of the plane, as usual, playing poker with the guys. Everybody was in a good mood. And why not? We were the Edmonton Oilers, kings of the National Hockey League, the best team in the world. We had won two Stanley Cup championships and were on the way to a third. We'd just wrapped up another successful road swing with an easy 7-4 win over the Jets in Winnipeg and were headed back to Edmonton.

It was going to last forever. At least, I never had any reason to doubt it as I thumbed through the cards. That's when I felt the tap on my shoulder and looked up to see our coach, Glen Sather, standing in the aisle.

Uh-oh! I thought. What did I do now?

I'd been driving Slats crazy for nine years. The Oilers didn't get any angel when they had acquired me. Through the years, Slats had probably given us a thousand curfews. I figure I missed 999 and he'd caught me every time.

"I've traded you to Hartford," Sather said, handing me a piece of paper. "Emile Francis is their general manager. Here's his phone number."

Much later, when the shock wore off, I recalled how Slats

had been called off the ice of the practice he'd run us through in Winnipeg that morning. Right in the middle of all the drills, he had gone into the dressing room to take a phone call. Who knows? Maybe he'd talked with Francis and they might have finalized the deal right then.

I must have had a real bad practice.

But my first reaction when Slats told me I'd been traded was to think he was kidding me. We had all learned through the years that what Glen Sather says and what he really means aren't necessarily the same thing. You've heard of reading between the lines? With Slats, you also had to listen between the sentences.

Like the time he invited us to "Fun Camp."

It was my very first training camp as a pro in 1978 and it was . . . well, it was different. For one thing, it was in Europe. Going over there for preseason training meant we would have to start camp earlier than the date agreed upon in the players' agreement with the teams, so we were all given a waiver to sign.

First of all, you've got to picture Slats' office. Big desk. Big chair. Dead birds. Dead fish. That pretty well describes it. The man is quite the outdoorsman, and he has trophies all over the place. I don't know if he caught them or bought them. But they were there, all stuffed.

"You don't have to sign this and go over there," Slats said as he held out the waiver across his desk.

Sure, we didn't have to go. But when you sit down and think about it, it's a little tough to make the team when you're not at training camp.

Besides, we were going to have to go to training camp sooner or later. And here was the chance for a free trip to Scandinavia. How were we going to turn that down? Especially after what Slats had led us to believe. We all got a letter from him about the proposed journey and he didn't even call it training camp. He called it Fun Camp, the most misleading title on any document I ever got from the Oilers.

The tip-off came early. We thought we'd be staying in Stockholm, with lots of bright lights and beautiful blondes. We wound up in some little town in the middle of nowhere, going through two-a-day practices and hopping on buses to drive to exhibition games at ice-cold arenas in other little towns. Nobody spoke the language. One of our players, Paul Shmyr, used to watch the Muppets on TV back home. One of the characters on the show was a Swedish chef. So Paul, speaking broken English with the stupid accent they'd given this puppet, appointed himself as the official interpreter for the trip. We never had a chance.

We did manage to get all of six hours in Stockholm while we waited for the "cruise ship" that Slats had said would be taking us to Helsinki.

"Listen, the cruise ship has two nightclubs," Sather had told us. "We coaches don't want to bother you, so we'll split up; management in one nightclub and players in another. Have a good time, guys."

Then we got on this "cruise ship" and found out it was a damned tub. It was some sort of converted ferry. No shuffleboard. No skeet shooting. I'm still surprised it actually floated.

They had us fished right in. Our "nightclub" that Slats had so graciously assigned to the players turned out to be a little wee bar in the back of the boat. To make matters worse, we were stuck in these little tiny rooms and the sea was up and down all night. Half the guys spent the night with their heads in a toilet.

But at least we all came back to Edmonton as Oilers. Now here I was on a plane with Slats telling me I was going to Hartford. Hell, he had to be kidding. I'd never played a shift of pro hockey for anybody but Edmonton, first in the World Hockey Association, then in the NHL. They were never going to trade me. Or so I thought.

Maybe they were kidding. Practical jokes had become something of a tradition with the Oilers when the trade deadline rolled around each season. Lee Fogolin had become a favorite target. I'd been having fun joking about trades at other people's expense for years. Perhaps this was the payoff.

Fogie was a solid defenceman, solid citizen, and general all-around solid you-name-it, but he was always a little jumpy whenever the trade deadline approached. So I'd always find a way to bug him.

I'd look up the name of a reporter in some other city, make

up some fictitious phone number that looked as though it might be from that city, then leave a message with the hotel operator for Lee to call the reporter. Fogie'd come in, take one look at the message and figure he'd been traded for sure.

Mark Messier and Fogie used to room together. One year, about nine o'clock at night on the eve of the trade deadline, the message light started blinking on the telephone in their room. It was my message, telling Lee to call some guy at a newspaper in Buffalo.

He was flabbergasted. He told Mark that he wasn't going to phone or talk to anybody. He just sat there in a state of shock. All of a sudden the phone rang again, and Mark almost had to pry Fogie off the ceiling.

Mark answered the phone, listened for a second, then told Lee that it was Glen Sather on the line, calling for him. Poor Fogie couldn't answer the phone. He was so scared, he'd lost his voice. Turns out Lee was going to do some woodwork in Slats' basement and that's what Glen wanted to talk about.

But this was no joke. And Slats sure as hell wasn't going to let me take a hammer to his rec room. It was only two weeks before Christmas of 1986, and I was leaving the team I'd joined in 1977. The team I thought I'd be with until the day I retired.

It wasn't the end. I finished that season with the Whalers and then suffered through as much of the next year as I could with John Brophy and the Toronto Maple Leafs. But a big part of me never left Edmonton. And the rest of me couldn't wait to get back.

2

Tuning Up for the Pros

I ronically, I wasn't in that much of a hurry to go to Edmonton in the first place. When I left my junior team, the Brandon Wheat Kings, for the pros in 1977, I had two options: Minnesota North Stars of the National Hockey League or Edmonton Oilers, then of the World Hockey Association. And if it hadn't been for Glen Sather, I'd probably have ended up in Minnesota.

There really wasn't much difference between what Minnesota and Edmonton were offering me so far as money was concerned. But the North Stars had a little hitch in their proposal. They wanted to offer me a two-way contract. If they didn't think I could play in the NHL, they could send me down to the minors and pay me less money.

The minors were the last place in the world that I wanted to be. You can get lost real fast and real easy when you play down there. I'd heard about it happening to a lot of guys before and was determined that it wouldn't happen to me.

But even at that, I wasn't too sure about passing up a chance at the NHL to go play for Edmonton in the WHA. There were some big names in the league, but who really knew how stable the WHA franchises were, or the whole league, for that matter. I wasn't too sure about a lot of things. Originally, I'd had a fellow named Frank Milne representing me but hadn't thought I was getting anywhere. So I'd switched over to Ron Simon, an agent who worked out of Minneapolis. He'd been recommended to me by Bryan Hextall, a former NHL player who was a friend of my junior hockey coach, Dunc McCallum.

Although I was reluctant about turning Edmonton down, Simon recommended that we give Slats one last "courtesy call" before I signed with the North Stars.

"Don't let Dave sign with Minnesota," Slats told my agent. "They'll send him to the minors. Tell him that if he comes up here, he'll play on the big squad."

"So why don't you give him a one-way contract?" Simon asked Slats.

Sather said he'd call back in five minutes. But it didn't even take that long. A couple of minutes later he phoned back to say, "Okay, it's done." So I caught the next plane to Edmonton and signed with the Oilers.

Little did I know at the time that the Oilers didn't even have a minor league team. Slats couldn't have sent me down anywhere even if he'd wanted to.

Among the first things to change was the ice time. I wasn't some overage junior, playing half the game or more every night like I did with Brandon. I was a rookie pro and Slats wasn't taking any chances.

Sather would look down the bench, see me and think, Okay, we've got a five-goal lead and there's only thirty seconds left in the game. I guess it's safe to put Semenko out there now. He won't tie it.

But it was great. I was in the pros, and at twenty years old I saw my life change overnight to one of sheer luxury. I never minded riding the buses in junior hockey — I had a lot of fun on them, to be honest. But there I was, just a few days out of Brandon, getting on an airplane with the Edmonton Oilers to fly to Houston for a game. With a three-hour stop in Las Vegas on the way! Perfect.

Smokey McLeod was the ringleader, I think. It was kind of hard to tell, because all the veterans seemed to take off for the exit at once as soon as the plane rolled up to the terminal. Smokey might not have led the charge out of the plane, but he was the first one to the taxi stand. I remember that clearly because I was tagging along right behind him and hopped in for the ride.

We headed for what's now Bally's, the first casino I'd ever seen. I'd learned how to play a bit of blackjack on the buses during junior hockey days. But here in Las Vegas they had all these signals for cards and everything. I didn't know exactly what signal to give them for another card or just what to do when I didn't want one, so I just stood there and watched for a couple of hours. There was no way I was going to embarrass myself in front of those guys. Besides, at the time it was thrilling enough for me just to be in a place like that.

But if I looked like a real hick in Vegas, you should have seen the rube who showed up with number 27 on the back of his Edmonton uniform in Houston.

At the Houston arena, they had these massive television screens up on the wall at each end of the rink. They were great big things, and I'd sure never seen anything like them before. I hadn't been out of Brandon for a week yet.

So I went out on the ice for my first shift and was lining up behind the centreman. That's when I looked up and saw our team on TV. Hey, this is great, I thought. Then I saw me! At least, I thought I did. I'd never seen myself on TV before, so I wasn't too sure. I moved my right elbow a bit. Sure enough, the guy on television moved his elbow. Then I raised my left hand and scratched my ear. The guy on TV did that, too. Yup, sure enough, it was me.

But while all this was going on, they'd dropped the damned puck. The play had gone from the face-off circle into one corner, around the back of their net and was on its way up the far boards toward our end of the rink. Guys were swirling all around me. And I was at a dead standstill, scratching ears and wiggling elbows while I watched myself on this big screen. I guess it only took about five seconds for the wake-up call to arrive, but when I got back to the bench, I felt like I'd been out there for an hour.

There wasn't anywhere to hide. I just had to sit on that bench and feel foolish. The parting advice Dunc McCallum gave me in Brandon started to sink in.

Dunc McCallum's gone now. He died of cancer in 1983, far too young. Dunc was more than just my coach with the Wheat Kings. He was a friend and an inspiration. I caught the habit of getting into shape before I ever had to report to camp from Dunc, who was still playing in the WHA when I first went from Winnipeg to Brandon. A lot of pros used to spend their summers in that area of southwestern Manitoba and they'd come out to the Wheat Kings' training camp so they'd be ready to join their own teams. I ended up going back to skate with the young kids in Brandon for a few years every summer.

It's odd, but the one thing I remember best about seeing Dunc when he first skated out to join our practice was his Houston Aeros gloves. I wasn't used to seeing anything of that quality. Compared with the stuff we were using then, those were pretty good. I thought, I could score wearing those things. That was my trouble all my career. I'd get going along nicely and everything would be fine when all of a sudden I'd get this notion in my head that I was a fifty-goal scorer.

Dunc taught me that there was more to hockey than this junior career. I'd never even considered that. When Brandon put me on the list to play junior, it was exactly like the feeling that came later when I learned I'd been drafted by the NHL. My parents were excited. I was excited. It was the ultimate to play in the Western Canada Hockey League.

Dunc knew a lot of guys who used junior hockey as an excuse to quit school. They'd come, play for three years and it'd be a tough roll of the dice whether they'd ever make it anywhere.

I had finished grade 11 in Winnipeg. But my parents insisted that I keep up with my schooling while I was in Brandon. If I'd quit, they'd have made me come home. But why would I have ever wanted to quit? The time off was great. I split my grade 12 into a two-year program, because there was no way I was going to be able to take a full load at school and play hockey, too. We'd always practice in the afternoons and I'd take my classes in the mornings, provided we were in town. The teachers at Crocus Plains High School were great. No hassles, even though I didn't dazzle anybody with my grades. Back then, when we'd go on the road for a week or more, I wouldn't see a book from the time we left until we got back home. At least, not one that didn't have a lot of glossy pictures.

I got through it somehow. My graduation ceremony was a little different, too. I don't look good in those hats, so nobody had to give me my diploma. I just went into the secretary's office, picked it up out of a pile on her desk, and bolted.

Whenever we'd get the chance, we'd try to get Dunc to tell us what it was like to be a pro. We could see how he was living. He was very comfortable, had a beautiful home and a lot of property, and was raising Simmental cattle. The stories he'd tell about his friends in the WHA and the cities they went to... hey, I was used to Medicine Hat and Flin Flon. It gave me something to shoot for.

When the 1977-78 season began, I was a second-round draft choice. And I was fed up. Minnesota North Stars had picked me in the second round of the 1977 NHL draft, but they weren't going to pay me what I wanted. As a matter of fact, their first offer was a three-way contract of $8,000, $15,000, and $30,000. The last thing I wanted to do was be playing for $8,000 somewhere in the minors.

Houston Aeros had been the first to get my WHA rights, drafting me in 1977. But I never got there, because of a financial squeeze. The Aeros had to spend a bundle to sign André Lacroix to a huge contract, and suddenly I wasn't in their plans anymore and they traded my rights to Edmonton. But it didn't look like the Oilers were going to pay me what I wanted, either.

So I held out for the first six or seven games and planned on spending the season in Brandon as an overage junior. I figured I could get a lot of ice time with the Wheat Kings and that I might even get paid a little better than the rest of the guys in Brandon.

I'd had no choice but to get used to living on something less than what you'd call a fortune. When I'd started there in 1974 with their Tier II team, the Brandon Travellers, I was paid $25 a month. For some reason, they'd split it, unevenly, into two paychecks. We always enjoyed the second half of the month, because that's when we got a $15 check. The extra five bucks went a long way.

During the next three years, I'd managed to build my salary up to $200 a week. That would stretch pretty far, though we still cut a lot of corners. We used to hang around the Trifon Pizza store, crying about being broke every night until the owner, who was a big Wheat Kings fan, would finally take pity and give us a free pizza. Then there was summer work, when you could put a couple of hundred bucks into the bank.

Somehow, the money never seemed to run out. I didn't know any better about making $40,000 or $50,000. I knew how to live within my means back then. Somewhere along the way, I got forgetful.

Those seven WCHL games I played before turning pro in the fall of '77 were among the more enjoyable games I ever played. They certainly were the most unusual: I scored ten goals and had five assists. I was the big star, playing all I wanted and doing things I had never done before. Or since.

All the ice time was great, but it sure felt strange. In my first year at Brandon, when I was seventeen, I'd only be called up for a couple of games with the Wheat Kings here or there. Usually when the New Westminster Bruins came to town. They used to play a real physical game and I'd get the call to come up and sit on the bench, just in case something happened.

I really enjoyed it, though. After the outdoor rinks and the little indoor neighborhood arenas I'd played in, junior seemed like the pros. A 5,000-seat arena was really big time to me then.

But even when I made the Wheat Kings' roster the next year, I didn't get to play a lot. I was a fourth liner who did a lot of fighting. And there was always somebody there to fight. In junior, you only have a short period of time to make the scouts take notice of you. It was the same in Tier II. It's the same anywhere. Guys want to get to the big time. So if they're not goal scorers or defensive specialists, they had to be fighters and fill the tough-guy role. And the best way to get a reputation was to fight the top guns.

There were lots of them around until my final year of junior. One of the best was Barry Beck, who played with New Westminster. We had some sort of unofficial agreement, I guess, because we never fought each other. When things got crazy between Brandon and New Westminster, Beck and I would more or less stand around together and let everybody else go at it. We oversaw the whole thing.

But there was only one Top Gun in those seven games I played as an overage player. And that guy was me. People gave me so much room during those seven games that it was just like public skating.

It didn't take long to get a reputation as a fighter because I was doing a lot of it. Word gets around pretty quick. In junior everybody talks. You'd be sitting in the dressing room or having a pizza and somebody would say, "Hey, do you know this guy? Ever seen him fight? How tough is he?"

So if you did this to this guy and that to another guy, word got around in a hurry. It didn't take long for people to back off a bit. Once you get that reputation, it goes a long way. Besides, I never worried about anything. Things happened so spontaneously that I just let them happen and worried about them later.

One night there was a near riot in Regina. I was involved in one of those postscuffle shouting matches and was half-way out of the penalty box to start fighting again when I looked across the ice and saw Dunc motioning at me to stay in the box so I wouldn't get suspended.

On that one night in Regina, for what was probably the first time in my career, I figured I'd abide by the rules. I stayed in the penalty box. For about a minute. Then one of their guys ran our goaltender, and in my book, that's a whole lot worse than leaving the penalty box.

So I made a beeline across the ice to this guy, grabbed him, punched him a few times, and had him down where I could bang his head on the ice, when I looked up at the Regina bench. Their coach, Lorne Davis, was going crazy.

His players were holding him back. He had his sports coat off, his shirt was ripped, and his tie was half off and he was still trying to get on the ice. I didn't care. I told him to come on ahead. What was he going to do on the ice with a pair of street shoes on his feet?

Next day, Lorne ripped me in the Regina papers. He said I should be thrown out of the league. He said that I belonged in a league where I could play against men, that I shouldn't be in junior hockey, beating up on seventeen-year-old kids.

That was fine for him to say. But how was I supposed to know how old someone is? Besides, what difference did it make? He's on the ice, isn't he? I was seventeen at one time and the older guys came after me.

Lorne became a scout for the Oilers and we've since become good friends. But I've never seen anyone as outraged as he was that evening. He wanted a piece of me real bad.

So, it turned out, did the pros. While I was coasting along in Brandon, things started looking a little better for me in both Edmonton and Minnesota. The pros seemed to want all the tough players they could get their hands on at that time. They were drafting a lot of the big players out of the Western Canada Hockey League. Scouts were always hanging around to watch us play in that league, a rough grooming ground where the schedule was long, the road trips were gruelling, and the fights were almost endless. The rugged Philadelphia Flyers had just come off consecutive Stanley Cup championships, so their style was prominent in the pros and a lot of teams were looking for big, aggressive forwards. I was in the right place at the right time.

My last game turned into one of those classic defensive battles that you get in junior hockey. With a couple of minutes left to go, we were ahead 9-8. I had three goals and a couple of assists, but couldn't be satisfied to let it go at that.

With about five minutes left to play in the third period, for some reason I still haven't figured out, I decided to take a running, flying leap at some guy in the corner. I didn't know who he was. I still don't. But I crushed him and they gave me a double minor for elbowing.

While I was in the penalty box, the opposition came back to score a couple of power-play goals and win the game 10-9. I wasn't worried about it, though. We were playing before the hometown crowd. They still named me Player of the Game and gave me a real nice kit of Brut shaving products.

So there I was after the game, sitting in my big corner stall that was reserved for the stars. It'd been Billy Derlago's the year before, but I'd claimed the space because he'd gone to the pros.

I was sprawled out, thinking about how great a hockey player I was and opening up the kit they'd given me when McCallum walked into the room, mad as I ever saw him get. He knew I was going to sign with either Minnesota or Edmonton within a matter of days, so he passed on a bit of humbling advice.

"Semenko, I've only got one thing to say to you before you turn pro," Dunc screamed at me. "For all the good that stuff's gonna do you where you're going, you can take that perfume and shove it up your ass!"

3

How It All Got Started

The whole thing got started on the insides of my ankles, just as it did for any other kid from Winnipeg who learned to skate on those outdoor rinks.

I never thought I would spend eleven years in professional hockey: two seasons with Edmonton Oilers in the WHA then nine in the NHL with the Oilers, Hartford Whalers, and Toronto Maple Leafs. Not when I was a kid, I didn't. That sort of thing was beyond my wildest dreams.

I first played house league in East St. Paul, a municipality on the outskirts of Winnipeg. It was years before I ever played in an arena. Any arena. I was fifteen the first time I got to play in the Winnipeg Arena, during a local minor hockey all-star game. What a big deal that was! How many times had I gone to the arena with a bunch of buddies to watch the Winnipeg Jets? To get the chance to play on their ice was the thrill of a lifetime. All kids have dreams and I was no different. I dreamed of playing in the big leagues. But it was something I could never grasp. It never got to the point during the years I played junior that I'd wonder what I'd do if I didn't make it as a pro, mainly because I wouldn't let myself think that far ahead. I was too busy doing what I was doing to even think past junior hockey.

It had always been a day-to-day thing, even back in house

league, when you'd have your regular team to play on, then go try out for the various triple A clubs who would advertise the times of their tryouts in the newspaper.

The same group of us who grew up playing hockey in the winter would play baseball in the summer. And my dad coached both teams. We tried to play soccer for a little while, but that wasn't our game. There was a big empty field in our neighborhood and we'd all borrow our dads' lawnmowers and cut out an area that was much larger than our yards. We first made the field so we'd have a place to play football. But we got tired of that pretty soon and ended up using it to play hockey with a volleyball for a puck. We were always playing some sort of hockey somewhere or other.

In the summer, we were usually on our bikes most of the day. I think I spent almost as much time on those tires as I did on my feet. We'd say goodbye to Mom after breakfast and wouldn't see her until it was time for lunch. Then we were gone again till supper. But a day never went by when we didn't get the sticks out. We'd set up a goal in a driveway and take shots at one another. I don't know how my parents lived with the noise we used to make rattling pucks off the metal doors on the garage. If it was raining, we'd move the games down into somebody's basement. It was always hockey, in some form, even if we had to get down on our knees and play with a Nerf ball. I even invented a hockey game I could play all by myself. I'd go down to the basement, stand on one side of the room, and throw a ball at the far wall. Then I'd have to stop that ball before it could bounce back past me and hit the imaginary net. In my imagination I was both forward and goalie, and I played that by the hour. Won every game, too.

But if thoughts of an NHL career were far my mind when I went to that first tryout camp in Brandon, thoughts of fighting were even further away.

I didn't know what to expect. That was probably best. But I was all gung-ho, though leaving Mom, Dad, and my brothers Mark, Brian, and Brad wasn't easy. Mom took me shopping and picked out a whole bunch of new clothes for me. Those wild coordinating jobs. Then Mom and Dad drove me out to Brandon.

It wasn't that far away from home, only a couple of hours on the Trans-Canada highway. It certainly wasn't as difficult for me as it was for some of the guys on the team who came from places as far away as Victoria. Still, I was totally lost. I didn't know what to do, where to go, or how to register. When my parents left to go back home to Winnipeg, it started to sink in that I was on my own for the first time in my life. But you make friends quickly in those circumstances because everybody's in the same boat.

While I didn't know what was going to happen next, a couple of the Wheat Kings' "veterans," Dale Anderson and Gerald Stoughton, had a certain air about them. These guys had been to numerous training camps before. Two, probably. Maybe even three. Everything was old hat to them. Right away, I knew I wanted to hang around with them, and as it turned out, we did become good friends.

But that came later. First came the Test.

Normie Johnson was coaching the team then, and I guess he didn't want to waste any time seeing what the tall, skinny kid from Winnipeg could do. So on my first shift in our first scrimmage, they sent someone out to test me.

His name was Kim Spencer and he was my height. But while I would have had to put weights in my pockets to come in much over 175, he looked like he'd go 200 pounds, easy. Making matters worse, he had a five o'clock shadow, which was pretty intimidating on a guy his size. At least, it was to someone like me, who was only just beginning to shave.

"Wanna go?" he says.

This was all brand-new to me. I had never been in a fight before. And I'm not just talking about a scrap during a hockey game. I'd never been in a fight, period.

The world might not be ready for this news, but I'd always been a goal-scorer in the lower minor leagues. Certainly nothing of Wayne Gretzky proportions; Hockey Night in Canada never came knocking on my dad's door wanting to do a story about the ten-year-old scoring sensation from East St. Paul. But I was usually pretty close to the top in the team scoring races when I was young. At least, my statistics were never hurt by too many penalty minutes because in minor hockey, you didn't fool around. Down there, if you fought you were thrown out of the game and automatically suspended for the next one. I couldn't get enough hockey. We only played about twenty games as it was. It was beyond me to fathom why anyone would want to give up the chance to play hockey over a silly thing like a fight.

When I'd lived at home, I never had to fight any battles for my younger brothers. There was no time for that. We were always too busy fighting one another. It was a typical four-brother family, and I don't know how my mom ever put up with us. She always wanted a daughter, but it probably worked out well that Mom never had a girl. I really don't think the poor kid would have had much chance to turn out anywhere near normal with the four of us boys kicking around. Still, we never really pounded on one another. All it ever amounted to was a continuous wrestling match.

But here I was in Brandon with this guy in my face, dropping his sticks and gloves. So I reached out with my left hand and grabbed his jersey. From there, it almost seemed as if things were moving in slow motion. I looked at my right hand, and there it was going back and forth, back and forth, back and forth.

I'd watched a lot of games on TV and perhaps I'd learned something from all the fights I'd seen. But I don't recall learning any great secrets or thinking about some strategy. It just happened. I grabbed with my left and threw with my right and it seemed like I'd been doing it for years. It all happened so fast that before I really realized I was into this fight, it was all over.

I knew right then I was in for a life of violence. But the violence was confined to the arenas. In all those years of hockey, I never had a fight off the ice. Nobody ever came up to me in a bar and said, "Okay, Semenko, let's see how tough you are." Nothing even close to that ever happened.

That was nice, believe me. Wherever I went, no matter what environment I found myself in, people were satisfied to talk about hockey or just ask me how I was doing. And I'm talking about a cross-section of people that involves some pretty tough guys. Everybody thinks of bikers as being a violent group, a crowd who'd try to provoke me to fight. But I've walked into a bikers' bar and it never happened. In general, people have been really decent to me.

The exceptions, rare exceptions, are easy to *hear*, believe me.

Goon is not a pretty name. Not by any stretch of the imagination. But the one that bothered me most was somebody managing to turn Semenko into Cement Head. What amazes me is that it still happens, even though I've retired. A guy came up to me in a restaurant not long ago and said, "Hi, Cement Head! How's it going?" I swear he seemed like he was going to say "Dave" but stopped himself short to call me Cement Head as if it were my given name. He wasn't trying to be ignorant, but I don't need that. I told him I wasn't interested in anything he had to say and that I wasn't going to answer any of his questions. I'd been through all that when I was younger. I spent a good part of my career trying to prove that I didn't deserve that label.

I'd hear it on the ice every now and again, most of the time from the opposition bench, where I couldn't identify who was doing the talking. The rare times it came from someone on the ice, it was almost always from one of the smaller players. Then, I had no recourse. I had to ignore it. If I'd lunged at some little guy and shoved his words back down his throat, all I'd be doing was proving that he was right in the first place.

But I got other comments, too.

When you play hockey for a living, you live in this little world of its own. You travel with the team. In your hometown, you'll socialize together and go out for dinner in pairs. You never seem to mix with the general public at all. Same thing with the off-season, when hockey players will go on holidays together or spend their days in foursomes playing golf.

I knew I had to break away from that eventually, and the only way was by making friends outside the game. Maybe I did it at the time to prove to people that I could talk intelligently. Gradually over the years, especially when I gave up going back to Brandon in the off-seasons and started to spend my summers in Edmonton, I got to know a lot of people and they got to know me, too. There was no way they could get to know me while they were in the stands and I was on the ice because they only saw the one, limited side of me and would only read what was printed about Dave Semenko, hockey player.

But as I got to know more and more people away from the game, the one remark I heard more than any other was "But you're so quiet." Everybody was expecting some loud guy who was pushing everybody around, ranting and raving and having chug-a-lug contests all the time. It really threw them off when they'd first meet me, because I'm not the type of person I seemed to be on the ice.

Sure, there have been times when somebody might have had a few too many and said something ignorant and the initial reaction was to tell them to just screw off and leave me alone. There were times when that's just what I did, but only if I thought it was somebody who had no friends at all in Edmonton. The last thing I wanted was somebody running around town saying Dave Semenko's a stuck-up jerk hockey player who thinks he's great and won't talk to anybody.

I liked going out. People always asked me if I didn't get tired of having to sign autographs all the time. Didn't it ever bother me? Hell, I always knew it was going to bother me a whole lot more if it ever stopped.

When you did go out, you had to be a little careful. To some people, athletes make perfect targets. A night with Nick Fotiu taught me that lesson.

During my early years in Edmonton, a long-gone restaurant called The Sports Page used to sponsor a slow pitch tournament during Klondike Days in the summer. There was a whole bunch of Oilers there, and Nicky was one of a group of New York Rangers who'd come to play in the tournament.

Some of us from the hockey crowd went down to the Red Garter Saloon they'd set up in a Westin Hotel one night. That's the night I eventually paid a lawyer about a thousand bucks because I didn't witness a punch. I can thank my old friend Nicky for that one.

All I can offer you is hearsay. I was in another room and only heard the reports secondhand. But it seems Fotiu was sitting at a table when some guy came up and grabbed Nick's mug of beer.

"Hey, this is mine," the guy said.

So Nicky one-punched him. Just knocked him cold.

I didn't even hear about it until a day or two later. But all summer long I kept getting these phone calls from some guy with a British accent. The first time he called, he'd asked if I had "witnessed an accident in Edmonton this summer." I thought he meant a traffic accident and told him I hadn't seen one.

"No, no," he says. "I was punched out by Nick Fotiu. Did you witness it?"

So I told him I hadn't and thought that was the end of it. Either he remembered seeing me at the bar or his girlfriend recognized me, but for some weird reason this guy thought I'd be his witness. I told him to forget it, which is just what I did.

Then one day I was walking out of the dressing room to go on the ice during training camp when some guy handed me a summons. Now he was claiming I'd done it! He wanted to sue me for $50,000 because his face was a mess and he claimed his speech was screwed up!

So now he wants to nail me. Of course, it all came to nothing. But it cost me a grand or so to get a lawyer and go through all the bullshit when the only person I can remember being there was me.

That's why I would never put myself in that position off the ice. Besides, if I was out in a street fight and somebody beat the shit out of me, I wouldn't have wanted anybody to know. It's not something you'd brag about, that's for sure. There are so many people out there who will say, "I'll take a beating. This guy makes a lot of money, so let's go after him."

Off the ice, no fights. And even between the boards there were plenty of times when I didn't have to drop my gloves to get a point across. I've looked guys in the eye and said something like "Look kid, you've got a long career ahead of you. Are you sure you want to screw it up by fighting with me?" That's stopped more than a couple before they got started.

But before I put too much polish on my halo, let's accept the fact here and now that I never had a clause in my contract that would pay me a bonus for winning the Lady Byng

Trophy. And as long as I was in the league, Gretz's scoring records were safe.

When I first went to Edmonton, Slats had called me into his office and talked about the top tough guys in the NHL. He mentioned Larry Robinson as one of the kingpins at the time. He told me I could be number one in the WHA.

Fighting is the same as anything else. If you do it a lot, you stay sharp. It got to a stage where my fights were few and far between. I was pretty inactive. A guy like Kevin McClelland, who lives to fight, would get into it whenever he could. I didn't especially like to sit around thinking about fights and didn't go out of my way to get into them. If you check my penalty minutes from year to year, you'll find that I really didn't get into that many. At least, not by comparison with some of the other tough guys around the league. But once a fight happened, I usually came away from it feeling pretty good. The older I got, the more I could get away from fighting. Still, the stage of my career didn't matter much. When I did fight, I had to win. A draw was not good enough. Not for me personally or for my team. I was expected to win decisively.

But right from the start I was always just one punch away from becoming obsolete.

Larry Playfair almost landed that punch. I never really got hurt in any fight, and Playfair's the only guy who ever really stunned me. I remembered playing against him in junior hockey and he never bothered me. I could stand in front of the opposition net and he wouldn't really hammer on me. He played the game in a rather gentlemanly fashion. He didn't look that mean, but he was a tough player, and our inevitable meeting took place in Edmonton one night shortly after I'd come up to the Oilers. I wasn't that worried when I went in toward him. Playfair didn't have that intimidating look. But when I reached out my left hand and got a real good hold on his sweater, I knew right away that something was wrong. Larry wore a sweater that was about twenty sizes too big. It just came away in my hand. It didn't tie him up at all. In the meantime, he'd managed to get a real good grip on me. He was free and I was in trouble. He really stunned me. He got off a great shot and my knees buckled. A few games later, we had our rematch. We both knew we were going to have to get into it again. And it was a good fight. There was no clear-cut winner and afterward Larry just looked at me, said, "Good fight," and skated off to the penalty box. That was the type of player he was.

But I had no shortage of other things to learn in those early days. When I played junior, especially in my last year, I had the run of the rink. So I'd got into the habit of wandering off my wing every once in a while. In Edmonton, they wanted my toughness, but they also wanted me to play my position. It took a long time for them to drill that into me.

It seemed like I was doing nothing a lot of times. The play would be between the bluelines, going back and forth all night. In his own end, a winger should just watch the point. That might sound easy, but that puck is like a magnet. I'd be standing out there by the point, figuring I wasn't doing anything, so I'd cheat a bit and try to rush in and scoop a loose puck up out of the corner. I gradually learned that while I might not be doing anything much offensively, I could be preventing a goal. But to go through shift after shift where you never even touch the puck or go through a game where you never even begin to get tired at all was pretty frustrating. I always figured it wasn't enough. No, I thought I had to show something; that I had to go get that puck. More often than not, I'd end up screwing everybody else up while they tried to do their job.

In junior, size didn't matter all that much. A lot of the smaller guys fill the tough player role in junior hockey, where fighters come in all shapes and sizes. So occasionally, smaller guys who really had no business doing it would come at me. They felt compelled to do it and it made for a lot of one-sided battles. I knew what they were trying to do. The faces and the teams changed. But you could always spot the smaller, rambunctious guys who wanted to prove something. I knew, sooner or later, they were going to come after me. There wasn't usually much talking. They just give you a little shove. They'd say, "C'mon, let's go." And I was always ready.

That changed a lot in the pros, where the little guys were the agitators. They'd needle you, hoping you'd retaliate and take some dumb penalties. But they weren't going to fight you, which certainly never bothered me at all. By the time I got to the pros, I had become determined not to fight the little guys, anyway. In junior, though, I had a lot shorter fuse.

Dunc McCallum was the first coach who really made an effort to get me to hold back in some situations. But by that time, I was in my last full year of junior. By then, it was too late.

Later on, of course, Sather got into it. He loved it when I played tough, aggressive hockey. But it comes to a point in the pros when you've got to be a lot smarter about things and pick your spots so you don't hurt the team. He didn't encourage some of the stuff that I did. But he never told me not to fight.

There were nights when it seemed that if I fought, we won the hockey game. It seemed to shift the momentum of the game. I always wanted to think I could shift it another way, say by scoring the winning goal. But when a team's down and the game's really dead, a couple of big hits or a guy winning a fight can really fire a team up. It's not a matter of going out onto the ice and trying to take somebody's head off or making sure there's plenty of blood on the ice. It was more a matter of having someone get involved. If you're out there just going through the motions and aren't getting involved, you're not going to accomplish anything.

Sather stressed that and it worked. But I'd always forget why I was playing so well. I would be hitting, getting in the odd fight, and being a force out there. Then I'd think, Okay, I played it his way for a while. Now I'll try it my way. Let's dipsy-doodle. Sure enough, I'd be right back on the bench. I did that my whole career with Slats. The whole time, I'd get things going and then I'd refuse to play within my means.

Slats would say to me, "I'm not concerned with how many goals you get. Don't worry about that." Scoring just wasn't to be a priority for me; the Oilers had so many other people who could put the puck in the net.

You could spot the scorers by the boomerangs they carried. Back in the WHA there was no limit on the curve you could put on your stick. Naturally, I had to have a big bend in mine, too. I'm surprised I could carry the puck five feet with some of the sticks I used. I'd have that blade bent to almost a circle, with taped knobs the size of a globe at the end of the shaft.

I'd shave them. Put a different curve on them. You name it, I tried it. But after a while I got tired of all the diddling around, so I just got one pattern and left it. After that, no rasping or sanding or major alterations. I'd just wrap a knob of tape on it then go play. Paul Coffey always used to tell me, "Sammy, don't waste your time doodling with a stick trying to make it air resistant when you're just going to go out there and drop it on the ice with your gloves."

I could have gotten by right from day one just taking care of my own end, playing defensively, being aggressive, and if the occasion should arise, getting into it. But it's hard for a hockey player to get it through his head that scoring doesn't matter. I'm sure that even to this day if I was playing, I could go to camp with the rest of the guys and tell myself, Okay, I really don't have to score; all I have to do is this or that and I'll be all right. But I know that over the season my priorities would start to drift. I'd forget what got me there.

If you saw any improvement in my game those first few years, you must have been at our practices. During games, Slats wasn't letting me off the bench.

My first line in practice consisted of Slats at centre and our assistant coach, Bruce McGregor, on the other wing. Those were my linemates for the drills! I used to beg Slats, "Give me a break, will you. I'm never going to crack the lineup playing with you guys."

One day during practice I was going in against Paul Shmyr and was supposed to dump the puck into the corner. But since my buddy Paul was the defenceman, I decided I was going to beat him. I put on a little move here, another one there, and thought I'd slip right around him. I had him totally beaten. Right out of the play. But somehow he just managed to get the very edge of his toe out there. He touched the puck just enough to throw it off course. I was about one centimetre away from looking like Gretz. Paul couldn't have made the same play again on a bet.

But you should have heard Slats. Whenever Slats called me Semenk, then things were okay. But when he said David, I knew I was in trouble. Something was coming and it wouldn't be pleasant.

"David!" he hollered. "What the f--- are you trying to do,

David! He's been in the league 100 years. You're not going to beat him on a stupid kid's play like that. How many times have I told you, Don't do anything fancy. Dump the puck in." Shmyr, of course, was standing back in the corner, leaning on the boards laughing like hell. He knew if he hadn't been lucky enough to get just that little piece of the puck, he'd have been out there looking foolish.

Slats was always on me about the fundamental things. Conditioning. Skating. Picking the puck up out near the blueline when it had been slammed around the boards from the far corner. I always had troubles with that one. Mess used to do an imitation of me: he'd let the puck go by him about ninety miles an hour, then look back to see it if was coming yet. One day I missed a couple of pucks near the blueline and Slats decided he was going to help me out. He dragged me into the dressing room, grabbed one of his old pattern sticks from years and years ago, got the rasp out, and started filing a stick down carefully for me. Then he taped it up and handed it to me with a smile. "Here you go, Semenk. Try your luck with this."

I said, "Jesus, Slats, no wonder you never scored more than six goals a year using a puny piece of garbage like this."

I thought he was going to die.

For a while, I began to suspect Slats and the other coaches were trying to get me ready for the Ice Capades or some damned thing. They made me take power skating lessons, which really isn't something I'd have lined up for myself if there were any choice.

For reasons I've never been able to understand, Slats didn't think I was a gifted skater. But what does management ever know, anyway?

No matter, I ended up taking lessons. It was something I really dreaded doing. I thought it was something that only sissies would do. It reminded me of the days when my mom would send me off to piano lessons. Honest, she did. For five years! Can you imagine me with my music sheets in my bicycle carrier, riding down to Mrs. Hamilton's place to play piano? God, how I hated those recitals. That's what power skating felt like.

Everybody else would be in the dressing room, showering

and shaving. And there I was out on ice with Audrey Bakewell, taking skating lessons. Realistically, it was something that proved to be a big benefit in the long run. But at the time I sure didn't see where some of those stupid drills could possibly help. At least, I thought they were stupid. Then after a couple of months off in the summer when I'd start skating again, all these things Audrey had tried so hard to teach me would start to click.

But I hated it at the time. Practice would be over, all the guys would be heading off together for lunch, and there's Sammy, taking his skating lessons. I wanted to be with the guys. I didn't want to be following Audrey around. I felt foolish. You wouldn't think skating could be difficult for a guy who makes a living playing hockey. But take that stick out of our hands and most of us are lost. That's how I felt trailing around behind Audrey.

But the ultimate embarrassment was the inner tube, the brainchild of one of our early assistant coaches in Edmonton, Dave Dryden.

Dryden wanted me to practice bodychecking along the boards. Good, I thought. At least this would help me put my size and strength to good use. Little did I know. Dryden put a sweater over an inflated tire tube, then attached the tube to one end of a hockey stick. He'd hold out the stick against the boards and tell me to hit the tube.

The guys would stop practice and cheer whenever they saw Dryden bringing that stupid tube onto the ice.

"Oh boy, more hitting drills for Sammy," they'd laugh.

What a goofy drill! If I was just a little bit off balance going in or hit that tube at the wrong angle, I'd come bouncing back off the boards like a puck off a post and land flat on my ass. The guys loved it.

One day I figured I'd had about all I ever needed of that stuff. So I drove a nail halfway into the butt end of my stick. When Dryden brought out his dummy, I took one run at the thing, drove the nail right through the tube and skated away with a smile on my face while the son of a bitch went flat at the end of Dryden's stick.

4

Grab with the Left...

Not very many people would admit they go to a hockey game to see a fight. But not very many turn their heads away when one breaks out. Do you? Violence and gore attract attention. It's human nature. People don't speed up to go past a traffic accident.

Hockey's a fast game and tempers flare real quickly. People like to get an elbow up or a stick in there. There's always a little extra going on. That's when the fighting comes in. It only lasts a little while. You don't see a lot of guys getting hurt from it. The majority of times you'll get your equipment messed up and that's about it.

In hockey, enforcers are a deterrent. Like the United States and the Soviet Union, each with its nuclear weapons. Hockey players, regardless of their roles, aren't as stupid as trees. We get to know who does what for each team. And we know that almost everybody's going to have a tough guy. Or two.

Not that a team's going to go out and get somebody who can remove a kidney or another vital organ with a flick of a stick. You just have a player around who can deliver the message: don't mess with us, we won't mess with you. That's the way the tough players' role should be, and it's something you'll never take out of the game.

How can you? If all the league governors and general managers got together to say "No more tough guys in this game," it would only be a matter of time until one team put one out on the ice. And before you knew what was happening, every other team would have one of their own to neutralize him.

Ideally, the situation can be neutralized without punches being thrown. That's hockey. That's strategy. There's no strategy involved in fighting. Not when you're wearing skates.

When I played in Brandon I met Rocky Addison, a former Manitoba middleweight boxing champion who'd coached the Wheat Kings at one time. He was a friend of Dunc's, so we'd often see him around our room. Whenever we'd run into each other, Rocky would always try to get me to work out. But I thought I was doing all right on my own. He didn't like the way I fought, though, and I figured I had better listen to what he had to say, even though my style seemed to be pretty effective.

I never got into a lot of toe-to-toe fights, where you'd take one then give one. I didn't believe in that. It always seemed like an unnecessarily painful strategy to me. Almost all my fights would either be in tight, where there was a lot of pushing and grabbing, or else they'd be held at long range and over real quickly. My theory was that getting five minutes for a wrestling match was a total waste of time. I always like to stand back and go right at it.

Rocky didn't believe in haymakers. He wanted me to shorten my punch to six inches! I couldn't figure out how a punch was ever going to do any good in six inches. I figured, no thanks, I'll bring it in from left field. That'll be more effective.

Years later Rocky helped me work out before I boxed a three-round exhibition with Muhammad Ali. I'm still not sure how all that came to pass. Anybody who might think Mark Messier is a real character should meet his uncle Larry. He was always promoting something. When I first met him, he was going to bring up a bunch of movie stars from Hollywood to play the Oilers in a charity floor hockey game. That's how it all started. But like I was saying, Larry Messier is something else. The floor hockey somehow turned into a fight, with me getting into the ring with Ali.

A group of us were having lunch one day when Larry

looked across the table and said he could set up an exhibition bout between Ali and me. I didn't know if this was some sort of scam or what. But the next time the Oilers were in Los Angeles to play the Kings, Messier brought Ali down to our practice.

Right from the start I was really scared about how this was all going to come across. When I first was taken over to his house to have a meeting about this proposed fight, Ali came walking into the room, put his hands up, and said, "Okay, show me something."

I threw a few combinations and Ali said, "Don't worry, kid, we'll make it look good."

Then he left to take a nap!

Next thing I know, Larry's talking about having Ali come after me with a hockey stick that had a boxing glove on the end of it. That's the last thing I wanted. As time went on and the fight date drew closer, I became more and more worried that this might turn into some sort of comedy act.

I tried to train seriously. Rocky had phoned and offered to come up and help me train. We only had a one-week training camp. But it was tough. They'd only just introduced Happy Hours in the lounges in Edmonton and the first thing Rocky did was put me on the wagon. Two-for-one sodas are not my idea of a Happy Hour on a hot June afternoon. But I wanted to put on a good exhibition. I didn't want this thing to be a farce. But Ali hadn't said very much. I didn't know what he was apt to do.

I was so relieved when it was all over and things had gone well. We got a really good response from the crowd. Ali had done a little clowning around in the ring, but only his usual stuff. I was glad to get it over, though. After all, I had to live in that town. Wouldn't you know it, but I was the biggest clown of all. Fortunately, not many people noticed.

I didn't know what I was supposed to wear and didn't have a boxing wardrobe kicking around the house. I didn't have boots like Ali, so I got a pair of old black high-top runners. He had his zippered sweat suit to wear into the ring. I wore a crimson-and-silver terry-towel bathrobe. We hadn't even thought about it, but I'd been wearing the robe when they laced the gloves on me. So there we were, standing in our corner with the opening bell about to ring and I couldn't get the damned bathrobe off over those great big sixteen-ounce boxing gloves. So Rocky stood real close to me, trying to block out everybody's view, while he hacked the sleeves off my bathrobe with a pair of scissors.

Rocky had always been a big Ali fan and had brought a whole bunch of films of Ali fights for us to watch while I trained. Rocky said Ali preferred to move to his right, so I should try to make him move left. Somehow, I think Ali just might have found a way around me. I trained hard, though. Too hard for an exhibition, I guess. During our training someone from Ali's entourage had watched me work out. I was pounding away at the pads, punching hard, when the guy came over and told me, "Listen, make sure you don't do something stupid, like try to take the champ's head off." I guess there was a time or two when he was kidding around with his Ali shuffle or yapping to the crowd that I could have suckered him pretty good. But I might have knocked him down and hurt him. Far worse, he might have got up and become very violent.

It was an amazing experience to meet him, though. When the cameras are rolling and Ali is putting on his show, he can be one hell of an actor. Yet he can be so quiet and totally different when he gets away from the ring and out of that spotlight. Still, you could tell that something had to be wrong. The day after the exhibition they had a private barbecue for the people involved, and of course, everybody wanted his picture taken with the champ. I got to see a lot of those pictures, and it's amazing there are so many in which Ali's eyes are closed or he seems to be just looking off into space. I don't know if he was on tranquilizers or some other sort of medication, but he wasn't the same person I'd watched on TV and seen in so many interviews. You knew something had to be wrong with him.

I guess that's what comes from years of catching too many of those short, quick punches Rocky always wanted me to throw. But the boxing ring was a totally different world from the hockey rink. My fighting was done on ice, where you'd grab with one hand and swing from as far back as you could with the other. There's no technique to that.

I'm sure when the fans look down at a couple of hockey players who are ten feet apart, feinting around at each other, they might think the players are jabbing with their left hands. Look again. You'll notice the players have their left hands open, like claws. They're really looking to grab the other guy's sweater rather than jab. Grab with the left, hit with the right.

But you've got to be careful. I remember Mike Foligno and Pat Price squaring off once. That was fun to watch, though I don't think Pat enjoyed it much. Foligno was standing up like he was a right-handed fighter, just lobbing his left out there for a grab. Poor Pat didn't realize it, but Mike was really left-handed. Pat got all caught up with watching that left hand. All of a sudden Mike switched around, grabbed him with the right, and started throwing his big lefts. It was a mess.

Most fights aren't. With the equipment today, you do more damage to your knuckles than anything else. How are my hands? Ask me when I'm sixty. By then I'll probably be able to feel every bone in both fists. They've taken a fair beating over the years. There were lots of times when one of my hands, or both, would be so swollen that I could barely put my gloves on. But I had to, especially in junior where you never did get any time to heal. I'm not sure just how many bones might have been broken in my hands over the years. A few, I guess. But the knuckles never were really broken. They just gradually got moved around a little, ground down and rounded. Helmets will do that to you. They're dangerous. Nobody should be allowed to wear those damned things.

A lot of people probably figured I was crazy for not wearing a helmet. They're probably right. But I was very fortunate. I got through my career without ever coming close to any serious head injuries.

I did wear a helmet during my first couple of years in Edmonton. We were in Regina to play St. Louis during training camp one night before my third season. I thought I'd take my helmet off, just for a change. I'd never worn one during a team practice session. And, as usual, I was one of those guys who always seemed to do a lot better in practice than I did in the games. So I figured I'd give it a shot without the headgear and I liked it. Helmets don't really inhibit you that much. I just seemed a little more aware of what was going on around me when I didn't wear one.

And in those days, it helped to be aware. They can say all they want about how Bobby Hull and his Swedish team-mates, Ulf Nillson and Anders Hedberg, playing that tic-tac-toe hockey the Winnipeg Jets made so popular. But don't let anybody fool you. Back in 1977 the WHA had more than its share of guys who were every bit as adept at slugging as they were at skating. It was a rough, tough league. Jack Carlson was in Hartford. Gilles "Bad News" Bilodeau was in Bir-mingham. Winnipeg had Kim Clackson. Quebec City had Curt Brackenbury. Cincinnati had a real dandy named Bruce Gregg. Remember the Paul Newman movie called *Slapshot*? There were three guys on Newman's team in that film called the Hanson brothers and the characters they played were the ultimate goons. They'd put tinfoil on their knuckles before each game. Two of those Hanson brothers were Jeff and Steve Carlson. Jeff was a tough guy for the old Minnesota Fighting Saints and Steve played for both Minnesota and New En-gland Whalers.

I found out just what I was in for during my first game in Houston. I was skating down the ice in Houston, minding my own business, trying not to look up at that damned television anymore. We were just nicely into the first period when I looked over and saw a teammate, Ron Busniuk, in a bit of trouble. Ron was poking around, overmatched with Houston's Cam Connor. Ron was a smaller defenceman who didn't have a reputation as a great scrapper. Connor wasn't afraid of anybody, but he had a reputation for being better with his stick than he was with his fists. So I stepped in. It really wasn't much of a fight. Two punches, that's all. I only remember it because it was followed by my first five minutes in a pro penalty box. They weren't the last, by any means. Hell, I almost lived in the penalty box on that trip. That game in Houston was a crazy one all night long. And from there we went to Birmingham, where they had what you might call a pretty rugged club. They were coached by John Brophy and were a pretty good mirror image of him.

Nobody had to ask me twice back then. Things happened with a great deal of spontaneity. The sight of blood really used to get me going. Especially if it was mine.

We were playing in Hartford when I first fought Jack Carlson. It had been a good scrap. He'd landed one or two. I'd landed a few more. The linesmen broke us up and we were standing around on the ice when I realized I was bleeding. That's when I lost it.

I couldn't get back at Carlson because the linesmen had us so far apart, but I had this overwhelming urge to do something. I looked around me for a Hartford player I could hit, and there were Johnny "Pie" McKenzie and Davie Keon, both within arm's reach. But hell, I couldn't hit them. They were just little guys. That's when I saw George Lyle standing right there beside them. He was a big kid and not really known for his fighting, but I couldn't help that. He was just unfortunate in being in the wrong place at the wrong time. I stunned him pretty good with the first one to the nose and beat on him pretty good for quite a while.

Clackson? Sometimes it felt like we spent half of our careers fighting each other. We went all the way back to junior days in Western Canada, when he played for the Victoria Cougars. The first time I saw Kim I didn't know what to expect. I'd heard all about him. His reputation was what you might call a little frightening, because he was supposed to be right off the wall. He couldn't be intimidated, no matter what. There were rumors flying around the league about the thousands of stitches his stick was responsible for. Guys like that scared me more than anything. You could pound on them only to have them come back later and cut your eyes out with their sticks. So it was something to walk into his building in Victoria for the first time, especially when he was nineteen or twenty and I still wasn't seventeen. We never fought each other during the time we were juniors, but we made up for lost time when we both moved up to the pros.

All hell broke loose one night when Clackson cut Gretzky, who'd been cruising through the crease. I was away from the play but Mark Messier was in the neighborhood, so he went right after Clackson. The linesmen had them separated and

Clackson was in the penalty box when I got into it with Russ Anderson and we were sent off, too.

The fights were still going on out on the ice. I sure wasn't prepared to just sit there in the penalty box like a statue, so I said to hell with it and hopped out of the penalty box, turned around, and invited Clackson to come out. Now here I am, standing at the door to their penalty box, trying to get at him. But while I'm throwing lefts at Clackson, Anderson's trying to grab my arm. The two of them were both trying to get hold of me and drag me into their penalty box!

Meanwhile, though I didn't realize it, a brawl was breaking out behind me. Anderson saw it and went to find someone to fight. That left Clackson and me all alone. He wasn't going to back down, so we went at it. The first thing I did was get his helmet off so I wouldn't hurt my hand at all. I managed that and we thrashed around a little more. Then the linesmen came in and broke us up.

At that point, nobody was bothering me and everything seemed evenly matched, so I just watched the fight. But about a minute later Clackson wanted a rematch. He'd found his helmet, strapped it back on, and damned if he didn't come right back after me. So we went at it for a little while longer. I got the helmet off him again and got on him pretty good until the linesmen came along and separated us a second time. So I figured it was over. But guess who's got his helmet strapped back on, looking for another piece of me? Clackson. We went at it a third time. Three times during one fight. That had to be a record. My hands were sore from hitting this guy on the head, though you'd never know it from looking at him. He looked so innocent, with that baby face of his that was almost impossible to mark. I had one good fight against him in Winnipeg when I got a lot of punches in and thought I'd rearranged a few features rather drastically. Yet when we lined up to play the next game, there's Clackson without a mark on his face.

By the time the Oilers moved into the NHL, I'd met just about every tough guy there was in the WHA. All hockey players read the NHL summaries in the paper every morning. It's a small world and you like to know what's going on. My fights during those WHA days got a lot of ink, particularly the one where I ended Rosie Paiement's career. He came at me from the back and I got him pretty good with a punch that unfortunately did a lot of damage around his eye. Another time, I gave it to Rick Vaive pretty good, and the wire services picked up the picture. Either that or Slats delivered it to them. One way or another, pictures of that fight got into a lot of newspapers all around the country. So starting in the NHL wasn't exactly like going back to scratch again. There was no long line of guys waiting to test me out. Which was fine by me because my attitude had never changed: I'd much rather just play hockey. I'd far sooner contribute with a goal or an assist. But I had a job to do, and there were plenty of other guys who would be glad to fill the role if I didn't.

Some nights, when for any variety of reasons fans might have gone to the rink expecting lots of rough action, nothing would happen. Nothing at all. Even in the second game of a back-to-back series, after the first one had been pretty aggressive. How could things cool down so fast? Easy. There are so many quick emotional changes in hockey. You'll see two guys start pushing and shoving while they fight for a puck along the boards in a corner. The linesmen will jump in and separate the players, who look like they want to gouge one another's eyes out. Yet those same two players will stop for less than ten seconds, line up right beside each other for a face-off and, when the puck's dropped, stay clear of each other. You'll see that a dozen times, at least, in every game you watch. As a professional, you can't take the attitude that this guy did something to me that he shouldn't have and I'm going to get even, first chance I get. The opportunity doesn't always present itself. Besides, there's a lot more at stake than a personal grudge. There's a hockey game to be won.

Occasionally, though, you take a number. I took a few, including Vaive's. When he played for the Birmingham Bulls of the WHA, Vaive was a cocky young kid and was always yapping at me from over a linesman's shoulder. Little bugged me more than somebody who would yap at you like that only when there were people separating you from them. I especially hated it when the guy doing the talking was smaller than me, because there's no way I was going to get into it with someone half my size. People around the league caught on to that pretty quickly. I listened to a lot of jabber from little guys who knew they could get away with saying whatever they wanted.

But Vaive was the right size. He was perfectly acceptable. One night he really got to me with all this talking, and I remember saying to Ron Chipperfield on the way home after a game in Birmingham, "That Vaive kid just moved up to the top of my list."

I had to wait two weeks for the Bulls to come to Edmonton. But the next time they did, I was at the blueline when Vaive tried to push me offside by coming up behind me at the blueline and cross-checking me across my shoulder blades. That did it. I turned around and dropped him with one punch. Then I hit him again on the way down. And I gave him another one when he hit the ice. He was a vegetable after that.

But as much as I looked for that fight, I wanted to avoid the tussle I got into years later during the 1985 Stanley Cup playoffs in Chicago. Behn Wilson and I went at it in what had to be the worst fight of my career. I was powerless against him. I'd reinjured my right shoulder and didn't have confidence in my throwing arm. So I hung on to Wilson's sweater instead of breaking away and going toe-to-toe. The opportunity to break away was there. But I didn't take it. The way my shoulder was feeling, I figured Wilson's punches would be getting in a lot quicker than mine. I felt like I had two left arms and I sure wasn't going to get knocked out. The only sensible thing left for me to do was to get in close, hang on, and take some shots on the back of the head until the linesmen broke us up. I hated having to do that because it had always bothered me to see others hang on. Wrestling's a waste of time out there. It doesn't accomplish anything. The guys never said anything about that fight when we got to the dressing room, but I know it bothered a few of them to see me do that. I know Sather was pissed off. The normal thing would have been to go right back at Wilson again, but I didn't because the confidence wasn't there.

Slats didn't play me for the rest of the series against Chicago. And I didn't dress for the first game of the final against Philadelphia Flyers.

Before the second game of that final, Slats came up to me and said, "Are you ready to play the type of game that got you here?"

"Yeah, but I'm going to need something," I told him. Then I got some cortisone shot into my shoulder and went out to play.

I don't know how I hurt myself in the first place. The doctor said it might have been a carryover from my days in junior hockey. I remembered hurting it once when I was a kid. They said it was a slight separation, but I'd just get it taped up and keep playing.

It never did heal properly. It still clicks. Matter of fact, when I get out of bed on a cold morning, my whole body clicks.

5

Into the NHL

When the merger between the National Hockey League and the World Hockey Association went through in 1979 (the NHL still doesn't call it a merger, as if that matters), it really didn't make much difference to me that I was going to "make it to the NHL." I was going to play pro somewhere, and that's about the only thing that really seemed to matter a lot back then.

We were at the top of the heap in the WHA. We'd finished first over the season the year before and had played plenty of exhibition games against NHL teams. Any jitters about playing the established teams were long gone. I was all over any awe.

During the sixty-five games with the Oilers in the 1977-78 season and seventy-seven the next year in the final WHA season, I'd had my moments. The Hall of Fame nominations weren't exactly rolling in and I hadn't won the scoring championship yet, but I was always convincing myself that "next year" I was going to hit the twenty-goal mark.

Realistically, my major improvement back then was dressing a little better. I was still so delighted to be a pro that I didn't know how to act like one. I'm sure there were some fans who thought my number-one goal in life then was to win the WHA championship and the Avco Cup. Or to move on to the NHL and bring home the Stanley Cup. But to be honest, I was quite happy just to be driving around Edmonton in my new Trans Am, playing Smokey and the Bandit. Hell, my main priority was to get the T-tops off that car whenever the sun came out.

I'd met my heroes by then. And I'd already played against many of them.

As a kid, I'd grown up watching Gordie Howe play for the Detroit Red Wings and Bobby Hull, when he really was the Golden Jet, starring for the Chicago Blackhawks. They were my heroes. You couldn't get me away from the television set whenever those two teams were playing each other. I'd sit there, cheering for both teams and hoping for a tie because I thought Howe and Hull were so great that neither one ever deserved to lose. But the days of being a fan were long gone by the time I fought my way up through junior and joined Edmonton in the WHA. And so were the best days of Howe and Hull.

Bobby had signed his million-dollar contract to come over from Chicago to the Winnipeg Jets. But in my books, he was supposed to be a Chicago Blackhawk. Howe wanted to stay in the game long enough to play on a team with his sons. He came out of retirement in Detroit to sign a family package deal with the Houston Aeros.

By the time I got to the WHA, their hockey skills were waning, so it wasn't any frightening deal for me to play against them. I was so happy just to be there myself that I wasn't really concerned who else was on the ice with me.

Even at that, I'm glad I was wearing a helmet the first time I ever met Gordie on the ice. We were in Houston and the play had been whistled dead for a face-off when Howe skated past me real slowly. He had his stick out to the side, and rather than just pull it back in when he went by me, he raised it over my head. Almost. He clipped me, right on the top of my helmet. Not hard, mind you. Even if you'd been sitting in the front row, you probably wouldn't have noticed anything. But he ticked the tip of his stick right off my head. And know what? At the exact same time as he was clipping me, he said, "Oh, excuse me."

It was all so casual and such an easy move for him. Just a quiet little message from an old pro to a rookie. I thought,

Okay, I've been warned. And I never went near Howe again. You would be amazed at how valuable space can be when you're out on the ice playing hockey. The more elbow room people give you, the better. Gordie always guaranteed himself plenty of room. He'd had some serious injuries early in his career, and why should he have to go through any of that crap again? So if he wanted to send me that little greeting, fine and dandy. I knew where he was coming from. Besides, I figured it was great. Now I could go back to Brandon and tell everybody about the night Mr. Hockey tried to take the top of my head off.

Stories like that were part of Gordie's reputation. And I can tell you firsthand it's amazing what a reputation as a tough guy can do for your career. Look at me. Why, with all the extra room I had, I was able to score six or seven goals every year. It's astounding how a fellow's production goes up when he gets a little extra space. Same thing with Howe, though he does have a slight lead on me in career scoring. His hands were every bit as tough as mine, but they were a whole lot smoother.

Even the great ones had their off days, though. Not many, that's for sure. But even Gretz had a few of those days. The first time I ever played on a line with him, he was, to use an old hockey phrase, strictly horseshit. Slats had put Garnet "Ace" Bailey and me on Gretzky's line in Cincinnati one night shortly after Wayne joined the Oilers. We were the starting line and figured it was going to be great. We'd get all sorts of ice time in each period and we'd also get to go out on all the power plays. Wouldn't you know it, Gretz picked that night to have a minislump. Through almost half the game, he didn't do a thing. Not one thing. It got so bad that Slats benched him, meaning Ace and I got benched along with him. Of course Slats wouldn't think it was Wayne's fault. There's got to be something wrong with those slugs Bailey and Semenko, right? So Slats finally decided to put Wayne out there with another couple of wingers. By this time Gretz was so angry about having to ride the pine that he scored three goals in the third period.

I never spent any time even worrying about how Gretz went

about doing what he did. I used to watch guys my size and try to learn from them. Bobby Bourne, who played with the New York Islanders, was my height and almost as heavy. But he could just fly on skates. Toronto's defenceman Al Iafrate weighs in at 220 and he's one of the fastest guys in the league. I'd watch them and wonder what was wrong with my legs. What was I missing that these guys had? I never really tried to analyze Wayne. What he had couldn't be taught. I figured it was a gift from God.

He had so much patience. With a lot of us, we'd yell for the puck, and then if anybody did pass it to us, we'd throw it away the moment somebody came at us. We'd always hurry ourselves even though we knew we usually had far more time to react than we thought. Wayne's patience was beyond me. He seemed to know where everybody was. When I was on the ice, it always looked cluttered. There never seemed to be much room or time. Gretz made time and knew where the room was.

I got to watch a few games from up in the press box while I was recuperating from injuries. Looking down from the box is almost like looking at a chessboard. You can see things develop and spot all the open ice. From up there, it seemed like Gretzky was operating on remote control — that part of him was upstairs in the press box relaying all the right instructions to the other part on the ice.

I remember how both Kevin Lowe and I thought Gretz was full of it one day before a game against the Islanders. He said their colors screwed him up because the color combinations of their pants were so similar to ours. Right, Gretz, colors are a problem, are they? Kevin and I get to worry about Islanders like Clark Gillies, Bob Nystrom, Bob Bourne, and Dave Langevin. He worries about colors.

Then Gretz explained how he kept track of the traffic around him with quick glimpses. All he needed was a little flash of color and he'd know if anybody from the other team was right on him. But the similarity in pant colors forced him to really check out the situation rather than rely on a flash of color in the corner of his eye. We're talking split seconds here, but that's the level he plays at. I'm sure when he's in behind the net with the puck on a power play, with people all over him, he's probably counting down the clock at the same time to stay aware of how many seconds are left in the penalty.

You could see right from day one that he was special. But not even his presence could help us with the championship in 1979, the final year of the WHA. There was something strange about that entire season. We came so very close to winning it all before Bobby Hull and his Jets beat us to take the last Avco Cup title. It almost seemed that we were afraid to win, maybe because we wouldn't know how to handle it. We were caught in a whirlwind; everything seemed to be happening too quickly. Winning would have been almost too much to handle.

Then came the end of that league and the prospect of playing in the NHL. The WHA was like a "comfort zone." There were only six teams, but it was competitive and seemed secure. We spent a lot of time in those great cities. They were going to strip our team when it went into the NHL. We knew we were going to have to start over almost from scratch, that there would be a breakup of the "family" we'd developed. If the merger hadn't gone through, it wouldn't have bothered me at all. Especially since I knew I wasn't going to be one of the four guys the Oilers were allowed to protect. Even back then I couldn't really imagine playing hockey for anyone but the Oilers.

So right after the final series against Winnipeg in the late spring of 1979 seemed like a great time for some serious relaxation. A former teammate, Brian "Soupy" Campbell, had retired and bought himself a motel in Fort Lauderdale, Florida. There couldn't have been a better place and time for a guy to hop on an airplane for three weeks of rest and recreation.

It was a typical perfect day in Florida and I was out at Soupy's patio bar, playing shuffleboard with the locals for jukebox money. The phone rang. It was Lou Nanne, the North Stars' general manager, calling to welcome me back to Minnesota.

"Great, Lou!" I yelled over the music blaring from the jukebox. "Thanks a lot. I really appreciate you calling me."

Almost every word he'd said to me had gone in one ear

At age eight, with my first team, the East St. Paul Hockey Club in Winnipeg. I'm sitting, second from left. The coach: John Semenko, my father.

Proud to wear the Brandon Wheat Kings uniform in
1976-77.

No matter whether you're an offensive star, a defensive specialist or an enforcer, there's nothing sweeter than scoring a goal. Mark Messier (*left*), Paul Coffey and Glen Anderson offer me rare congratulations. (Edmonton Sun)

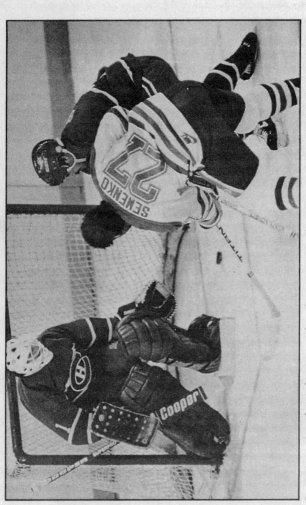

I pop in my 50th goal against the glorious Canadiens — 50th career goal, that is.
(Edmonton Sun)

and straight out the other. I'd listened to Lou, but only halfheartedly. No matter what he said to me, I didn't think there was any chance that I was going to wind up in Minnesota. I was right.

Nanne had explained that the North Stars still owned my NHL rights, but Slats eventually swapped Edmonton's second- and third-round draft picks in the 1979 NHL entry draft to the North Stars in exchange for my playing rights. Minnesota didn't come off badly in the exchange, using that second-round choice to acquire Neil Broten, a centre who won the Hobey Baker Memorial Trophy as the top U.S. college player in 1981. With the third-round choice, the North Stars got Kevin Maxwell, a centre who'd been the WCHL rookie of the year in 1979. And I stayed right in Edmonton.

Why was I so confident Slats wouldn't let me go? If the Oilers had wanted to get rid of me, I'd already given them lots of opportunities. They didn't get any angel when they called me up from Brandon. I'd already missed a few curfews and been fined for being a bad boy. But I always got a fair amount of my fine money back. Slats was good that way. Whenever I went into his office for our usual end-of-the-year meeting, he'd always give me an envelope with most of my fine money in it.

Knowing Slats, though, I'd imagine he probably collected interest off it in the interim.

We had more than a little fun with our fine money, especially during the early years in Edmonton, even though we always had to keep an eye peeled for Slats. When I'd first turned pro, Smokey McLeod was my roommate, but Slats wasn't going to put up with that for long because Smokey loved a good time as much as I did. Then Slats had me room with Ron Chipperfield, a steady and mature guy who probably would have been a stabilizing influence on me if he hadn't been traded shortly afterward. Then Slats paired me with Curt Brackenbury, who never, ever stopped fooling around. The closest I ever came to figuring that move out was to guess Slats wanted us both in the same room so he could keep an eye on both his troublemakers without having to worry about us being at opposite ends of the hotel halls.

Brack was a great guy to go out on the town with. He knew

how to have fun and he was more than delighted to teach me. We were the SWAT Team. Brack came up with that nickname, no doubt because the two of us weren't exactly the most subtle players in the game. Funny how nicknames will stick with you for years. As time went on, people nicknamed me Sammy. But a lot of the guys from those old WHA teams still call me Swat.

Brack and I also had our own SWAT headquarters in Edmonton. It was a strip club called Tracy Starr's. We'd visit quite often and bring a group of the guys over with us. The club didn't change its dancers all that often, so we got to know the girls quite well. There were never any major events. We'd just sit around, kill time, talk with the girls, and enjoy the scenery.

And it wasn't only the players who enjoyed a good time. Sometimes management even got in on the act when Larry Gordon, our general manager, would join us.

Brack and I were sitting around the old Sports Page restaurant having lunch one day shortly after a season had ended when one of our teammates, B. J. MacDonald, walked up to us. He had an envelope filled with fine money that had been collected from the team for this and that throughout the year and had decided he was tired of handling the cash, so he gave it to us.

We said, "Okay, we'll go to SWAT headquarters. That's the perfect place to start getting rid of all this." We put the word out everywhere we could think of, but it seems everybody had either gone home or had something else to do. Only three of the guys showed up — Brack, Larry, and me. But Larry was our GM, and he realized that by the unwritten rules of hockey teams, he was management and really didn't have any business partying on fine money that had been collected from the players.

"No problem, you guys," Larry told us. "Fine me."

"What for?" we asked.

"What difference does that make?" Larry said. "Just fine me a hundred bucks."

So we did. Then Larry threw a $100 bill into the kitty and the three of us had a helluva time partying away the fine nest egg. What a guy he was. We had a lot of great summertime parties at his place in Edmonton, a beautiful home that had a great swimming pool. For the life of me I don't know why, but Larry always asked us back. One time we ran out of red wine and I asked Larry if there was any more around.

"Sure," he said, "just go on downstairs and look in the cupboard."

I went downstairs, walked behind his bar, grabbed a couple of bottles, opened them up, and poured myself a little taste. Geez, it was the worst-tasting stuff you'd ever want to drink. No problem, I figured, Sammy'll fix this up right away. So I grabbed a big bowl. First, the wine went in. Then some 7-Up and soda. Slide a little sliced fruit in there, add ice, and presto! Wine coolers! Little did I know Larry had bought these wines at an auction. He'd spent hundreds and hundreds of dollars on the stuff. You should have seen the look on his face when I walked up, showed him the empty bottles, and said, "Hey Larry, nobody was going to drink that stuff, but don't worry, I fixed it up for you."

Larry had done a lot of travelling around the world and had some wonderful and extremely fragile souvenirs. Somehow, nothing was ever damaged. Except us. We were all supposed to show up early down at Northlands Coliseum to have our team picture taken one morning after we'd been partying. What a mess that was. Cars were coming and going in the cul de sac where he lived, and his neighbors weren't exactly the happiest people in Edmonton. Most times, in most places around town, people were happy to run into members of the hockey team. The party must have been a little louder than usual, though, because nobody was overly delighted to see us that morning. Certainly not on that block. Mark Messier, Kevin Lowe, Dave Lumley, Dave Hunter, and I must have looked like hell warmed over when we came wandering out into Larry's front yard about eight o'clock in the morning. We all stood around for a minute shooting the breeze, when somebody recognized us. Sure enough, every little kid in the neighborhood came running over, wanting autographs. And sure enough, every parent was standing on the front steps yelling to the kids, "You keep away from those guys!"

The five of us were not exactly the most impressive group when we all piled into my car. Mess wanted to drive, which was fine by me, so I dug into my prepractice kit that I always kept handy and pulled out the Visine, mouthwash, and after-shave. Everybody doused themselves with everything. But when we got to the Coliseum, would we have the brains to park out in the lot? Of course not. With all of us urging him on, Mess drove right down the ramp to the back of the building, had them open the great big door of the delivery entrance, then drove right up underneath the stands to the dressing room door. We were hanging out every end of the Trans Am, laughing like mad, just about to open the doors and get out, when who should come walking out of the dressing room and almost trip over the car? Only the team's owner, Peter Pocklington. And worse still, our coach, Glen Sather. We were dead. I have no idea what Pocklington's reaction was. None of us was looking at him. Slats was the guy we had to worry about, and he had the fire in his eyes. I can still hear him screaming, "Get that f------ car out of here!" We thought we were the big wheels. One scream from the boss and the grand entrance became the quick exit. We slid back into the car, burned rubber out of the Coliseum, and forever after parked outside in the players' lot.

At that stage of my career, I never really had much reason to pay attention to Pocklington. I don't think I'd ever said any more than hello to him at the time. He very rarely came into the dressing room. Every once in a while he would show up and toss out these little incentives. He'd slip us each a box of steaks, ham, and chicken from his Gainers meat plant when we'd do something important, like beat Calgary. Or he'd give us each a tailor-made shirt. Once a year he'd come into the room, usually just before the playoffs started, and give us one of his inspirational speeches. He was really good at that. He believed everything he said about positive thinking, and he could get the message across. I know I always listened to him. He wasn't telling us how to play hockey. He'd just talk about life in general, about dealing with trouble and remaining positive.

I'm sure he needed some power from positive thinking to get him through some long days after he traded Gretz to the Los Angeles Kings. What a deal that was. And what a reaction in Edmonton! I saw a woman driving a car with a tie hanging out of the back and a bumper sticker that read Husband in Trunk. After the Gretzky trade, I figured I could be a real hero in Edmonton if I drove around with a little gray beard hanging out the back of my car and a sign saying Peter Puck in Trunk. That would have got some applause.

I'll always be grateful to Peter for offering to help me once I retired from hockey. A few days after I'd left Toronto and returned to Edmonton, I got a message that Peter was trying to get in touch with me. That was a surprise. I never expected him to be phoning around town trying to track me down. He offered me a chance to learn the meat business through a management trainee course at his Gainers Packing Plant. I went to different meetings, but the guy I was supposed to talk to passed me off to somebody else. Then that guy would pass me off again. They weren't returning my calls. They didn't have anybody to supervise this program, and what I thought might be a short course began to look like it would take a couple of years. I didn't have to go through that plant more than a few times to realize it wasn't where I wanted to spend the hours from nine to five. But I thank Peter all the same. He didn't have to offer me anything, but he went out of his way to see if I could use some help with a second career.

Things had changed. In the beginning, I don't think he knew I spoke English. He just thought I was an idiot. It wasn't until I flew back from Toronto in his jet with Peter and his wife, Eva, that we ever really spoke. I'd picked up a six-game suspension for being first man off the bench in Calgary after I'd just come back from a three-game suspension for the same thing. We'd continued our trip to Toronto from Calgary and I'd gone on with the team as we awaited final word about my suspension. But when the team went on to Detroit, they said I might as well go back home with Peter. I don't think Peter was too happy with the prospect of my company. I'm sure he expected me to be nothing more than what he saw on the ice. He must have changed his opinion, though. A few days later, word drifted back to me that Peter had told one of the reporters that he thought I was "delightful."

Tim Hunter never called me that.

6

Aiming for Number One

The Oilers didn't rip the league apart during our 1979-80 debut in the NHL. The statistics from that year didn't indicate just how great the team was going to become. None of us realized it, either.

Still, it didn't take long for the message to sink in that we could play right along with the rest of those guys. We finished fourth in the Smythe Division that year, behind Chicago, St. Louis, and Vancouver, but ahead of Winnipeg and the Colorado Rockies. Our 28-19-13 record, .431 winning percentage and sixteenth place finish out of twenty-one teams wasn't much to write home about. But we made the playoffs and that's where we opened a few eyes, even though we only lasted three games in the best-of-five preliminary round against Philadelphia Flyers. Philly had won the Patrick Division that year and had finished the regular season with 116 points, forty-seven more than we'd been able to collect. We were supposed to be pushovers, the experts said. Not quite. Bobby Clarke scored after eight minutes of overtime, and the Flyers won the first game in Philadelphia. They put it to us pretty good in the second, winning 5-1. But when we came back to Edmonton, we took it all the way to double overtime before Ken Linseman scored for Philadelphia and sent us to the golf course for the summer. We'd held our own and it was a boost to get that close even though we were a long, long way from the championship. It was almost as if we were being groomed for the ultimate, that we were learning to walk so we could run someday.

I didn't exactly burn up the NHL that first year, not with just six goals and seven assists to show for sixty-seven games. I didn't get a lot of ice time and the only regular linemates I had were Slats and Bruce McGregor during practices. But when I did get out there, people left me alone. I only had 135 minutes in penalties all year, which is less than in each of my previous two WHA seasons and a far cry from the 265 minutes I racked up during my last full year of junior.

It hit me that the Oilers had a good chance to win a Stanley Cup during the playoffs at the end of our second NHL season. We'd picked up a bit during the regular season, finishing fourteenth overall. But in the preliminary playoff round, little Andy Moog stood on his ear in goal for us and we beat the mighty Montreal Canadiens three straight. Then in the quarter-final, we took the New York Islanders, who were in the second year of their run to four consecutive Stanley Cup championships, to six games. We made them work like hell to beat us, and that's when it sank into my head we were for real. We'd come close and had the chance for the upset. If ever we needed anything to make believers out of everybody in our dressing room, those two series in the spring of 1981 were what did it. The confidence grew from there.

Until those 1981 playoffs, thoughts of the Stanley Cup had sat away in the back of my mind somewhere. Until you get close, it doesn't seem realistic that you might actually win it someday. But now we were starting to realize that winning the championship might be more than a dream. I wanted that Stanley Cup ring so bad. We all did. The guys on the team who had one wore theirs so proudly. Cowboy Flett had his ring from the Philadelphia Flyers 1974 championship. Ace Bailey had his from Boston Bruins' Stanley Cup in 1972. To be like them — able to carry that conversation piece on a finger for the rest of my life — that meant more to me than anything.

In the back of the bus we'd talk about "if" we won the Stanley Cup, what it might be like and how we'd react. Of course, we always wanted to win it dramatically, in overtime of the seventh game. But it's easy to talk and we talked too much. We blew the division semifinals to the Los Angeles Kings in 1982, putting a damper on a great year in which we'd finished second overall in the league.

I don't remember Slats ever telling us we weren't far away. But I do remember him saying, "Wouldn't it be nice." Damned right it would be. And we all knew it. All our lives we'd sat around watching different teams win the Stanley Cup. Why not us?

Gretz was in the process of proving beyond any doubt that he was the greatest hockey player in the world. And with every game, it became more and more apparent that the Oilers weren't just a one-man team. Young players were starting to develop into champions and were finally starting to get some respect. Even from their teammates.

You'd think that a player like Paul Coffey would be pretty hard to overlook. After all, he's going to have a front-row seat in the Hall of Fame someday. But even though the Oilers' superscout, Barry Fraser, had been quick enough to draft Coff in the first round, sixth overall in the 1980 entry draft, nobody laid out the red carpet when Paul showed up for his first NHL training camp at Jasper that summer. At first, he didn't show his offensive skills, which we now know to be almost limitless. For the first while he stuck to playing defence. Or should I say, trying to, since at the time Paul's defensive game wasn't much better than my offence. Poor Paul — to this day he still thinks Doug Hicks, his defence partner at that training camp, had a conspiracy against him. Hicksy was a veteran defenceman who'd played for Minnesota and Chicago before coming to Edmonton. He knew his NHL days were numbered, and he was more than a little worried about his job. Paul is still convinced that Hicksy was trying to screw him up and make him look bad to the coaches by telling him the wrong things to do all the time.

I didn't even notice Coffey early in camp. And I wasn't alone. One day a bunch of us were shooting the breeze after practice and discussing up-and-coming younger players when somebody said, "Hey, by the way, who is our first-round draft pick this year?" There was Paul, sitting right at the table with us, all dressed up in his jeans jacket, chewing quietly on his gum. I think he felt so small he could have hidden in a thimble right then. Of course, when we did realize Paul was the first pick and that he was right there at the table, then we immediately made him feel part of the group. We ordered a round on the rookie's tab.

Coffey was worried about getting caught up the ice out of position and being sent back to junior hockey. He didn't think he was really going to make it with the Oilers. But once he got going, he got the same attitude as Mark Messier. He'd try things. If they didn't work, he'd get a lot of heat about it. He would hear it for not playing defensively. But he was convinced he was going to play an offensive defence and by trial and error he got the job done. It got to the point that Paul used to just laugh at guys who would try to chase him around the net when he had the puck. He called it Pac-Man. They could chase him all they wanted, but nobody was going to catch him and he knew it.

A few years later, Paul had his revenge on me for that day I hadn't realized he was our top-drafted rookie. We were tied 1-1 with the Jets late in a playoff game at Winnipeg when Slats sent me out for a face-off. I was as surprised as anybody about that move. Gretz won the draw, threw the puck back to Charlie Huddy, who slid it over to Coff. Paul let a slapshot go and somehow the puck wound up in the net. I'd gone to the front of the net right from the face-off, and I really didn't know whether the puck had hit me on its way in. It might have gone off my skate. It might even have gone in off Winnipeg defenceman Dave Babych, who was all tangled up with me on the top of the Jets' goal crease. But they credited the goal to me and it stood up to be the winning goal. After the game, the reporters were all over me. There was a great big bunch of them with cameras and microphones and notebooks, all surrounding me. I was in the process of telling them that I really wasn't sure whether the puck had gone in off me or not when one of the minor officials came into the room and yelled, "Attention! Attention! The winning goal has now been credited to Paul Coffey." I have never been left standing all alone more quickly in my life. The crowd of reporters just vanished. They were all gone immediately, rushing over to Paul's locker. So much for fleeting glory.

Messier was similar to Paul in so many ways. It took quite a while for everybody to realize that Mess was a very special talent. He was never afraid to try anything. He wasn't afraid of screwing up. He knew he was good but every now and again, he would try to do too much and it would cost us. But where a lot of guys might try something, fail, and never try to do it again, Mark always went back for more. If he insisted on doing something one way, then he was going to do it that way, period, until it worked. His attitude was "Hey, if it causes a goal against us, tough luck. I'll get two back." Mark had confidence. He knew that even if he did make a mistake, Slats was going to put him back out there on the ice. It wasn't just that he was talented. You simply couldn't keep a person with his competitive drive on the bench unless you had a chain. A thick chain.

You don't really see what Mark does to a lot of other players. The last thing you want to do is beat him clean on the draw. I've talked to centremen on other teams and they've told me how they never wanted to embarrass Mark, because if they beat him, he was going to leave a mark on them somewhere with his stick or his elbow. Mark has such a competitive fire in him and gets so caught up in things that I've often wondered if he realizes what he does sometimes. In a game I played against Edmonton when I was with Toronto, Mark was going down the boards and Dale DeGray turned to take him out. Mark laid DeGray out cold with a cross-check to the face. I couldn't go out there and make the score even by attacking Mark. DeGray had been a teammate for a couple of months, but Mark had been a great friend for ten years. I wasn't going to fight him. But a lot of people in the crowd probably thought all hell was going to break loose when I skated over to Mess while he was complaining to the referee about being given a five-minute major penalty. I'm sure there were plenty of people in that building who thought I might have issued some sort of challenge to Mark. Actually, I told him, "What's all the fuss about, Mark? You're complaining about five minutes and we've got a vegetable in our room!"

Mess doesn't fight often, but when he does, he's devastating. He's got a mean streak that's unequaled. You can't implant it in a player, I don't care if he's eight feet tall. It's a given.

Gretz is possessed in a different way. He wants to win so badly. He won't go the route of trying to intimidate somebody with a jab here or a jab there. He does it with the puck. People complain about his skating at times, but watch him in a race for a loose puck when there's a chance to score a goal. Not many guys are going to beat him to the puck.

Naturally, Gretz and Slats got along real well. And Slats always had time for Mark. But there was always something different about the relationship between Sather and Coffey. From day one, they just seemed to rub each other the wrong way. Paul didn't want to take a lot of things from Slats, and Slats didn't want to hear him whining about anything. So there was always a little friction. He got on Coff quite a bit and you could see that it hurt.

A lot of it was strictly personality conflict. But Paul was a defenceman and, let's face it, our team was hardly known for defence. That's why it was such a confidence thing for us once we got Grant Fuhr in the 1981 entry draft. We knew that with Grant playing in the nets, we could count on those big saves that can turn a game around. We knew he was going to stop practically everything, so we didn't have to worry. I've never seen anyone like Fuhr. He's got something special. You could pin it on his approach to the game, his catlike quickness, or any number of other qualities. What it adds up to, though, is this: he's impossible to beat. Under pressure, he never panics. He'll be standing in his crease and there will be four or five guys in there fighting for the puck. Things will be whirling and swirling all around him but he'll just stand back and watch. He won't react until it's absolutely necessary. A lot of other goalies would be down on their knees, fishing around trying to smother the thing. But not Grant. He'd just stand his ground, refuse to panic, and wait the whole thing out. I never could figure out how he could stay so cool.

As for some of our other defencemen, hell, I could never figure out how they managed to stay alive. Anybody who'd fall down in front of a shot to block the puck the way Lee Fogolin and Kevin Lowe would do certainly had my respect. You wouldn't catch me doing that. No way. The only way I'd ever slide in front of a shot would be if I'd given the puck away in our slot, in overtime, in the seventh game of the Stanley Cup finals. Maybe. The defencemen could lie down in front of them if they wanted to. But I liked to leave the shots for the goalies. That's why God gave them pads.

Fogie and Kevin had unbelievably high thresholds for pain. If Lee had a charley horse he'd be up all night, icing it and taking care of the injury. He wanted to be back out there playing the next night and he usually was. Lee played hurt a lot. Most of us, if we were hurt, would accept it and let the injury run its course. Lee and Kevin would force themselves to get better. Those guys were constantly diving in front of pucks and putting themselves in positions where they were going to get hurt, but you didn't see them missing too many hockey games, no matter what was wrong with them.

Other guys pull the parachute pretty easy. Little injury here? Another little pain there? Sorry, Coach, can't go tonight. But nothing was going to keep Lee and Kevin out of a hockey game if they could do anything at all about it.

It took far too long for Kevin to get the recognition he deserved. When Paul Coffey was there, everybody watched him. That's all they watched. But Kevin was always back there. And he was so steady, your quiet superstar.

I've never played defence, so I don't really know how difficult it is. Just watching it scares me. Being a winger is the easiest job of all the positions. You know where you've got to be in your end of the rink. You just watch your point. You don't have to run around. The centreman's got to be in the middle of it all, thinking about things like whether it's time to move in and help the defencemen. We wingers were pretty basic. We'd stand out there, watch our point and try not to chase the puck around.

But some of the stuff the defencemen have to do! When do they leave the net? When do they get in front of it? Is it time to charge the corner? And they have to be talking to their partner all the time because it's all over if they get the front of their net stripped of defencemen. So you've really got to be aware of everything that's going on. Until you realize that and watch it, you don't really appreciate what these guys are doing. It explains why they wire the puck around the boards and get everybody out of trouble.

As this kind of player and attitude became part of the Edmonton Oilers' package, the team grew stronger, position by position. And the coaching staff had grown right along with it.

Slats always had control of what was going on, but he'd get wrapped up in the game sometimes, especially early on. Having been a player, he couldn't avoid it. There were a lot of better hockey players than Slats, but few, if any, that were more determined. He stayed in the NHL for ten seasons, playing with Boston, Pittsburgh, New York Rangers, St. Louis, Montreal, and Minnesota. He brought the fire he'd shown on the ice with him when he moved back behind the bench in Edmonton. We would notice when he got excited and it got us going. It's amazing how a person behind the bench can control the mood of the players. You have to have someone back there with control or you'll end up going onto the ice and being as reckless as the person behind the bench. When I got to Edmonton, he'd just taken over midway through the previous season, going directly from player to coach. Over the years, he gradually moved away from his old self, becoming a coach who set an example. Ranting and raving at referees and getting bench minors all the time isn't much of an example. Slats learned to keep his cool and that's the way his teams came to play.

The assistant coaches, John Muckler and Ted Green, were two of the greatest people in hockey. You just had to respect and admire those guys. You had no other choice.

Teddy is one of the most enjoyable guys I ever met. As a player and then as coach, he also had that fire. He was always saying that he wanted to become a better person and control his emotions. Of course, we were always glad to help.

I remember Teddy telling me that among the things that most annoyed him were people interrupting him over dinner in a restaurant.

"I don't mind autographs, but it really bothers me when

people come up to the table and ask for an autograph while I'm eating," he told Pat Hughes and me.

The very next afternoon we were out for a team lunch after practice when some guy came over to the table Pat and I were sharing. He started asking questions about the team's record. The opportunity was too good to pass up.

"I'm really sorry, but I don't have the answer to that question," I told him. Then I pointed over to the table where Teddy was sitting all by himself. "But there's the guy who does. His name's Teddy Green. He'll be happy to answer all your questions. And while you're there, be sure to ask for his autograph. That'll make him real happy."

So over he goes. Teddy was bent over with his face in his plate, wolfing down the Chinese food. It was just like bugging a dog that had its bone. Teddy was all ready to light into the guy when he looked across the room and saw Pat and me laughing, so he gave his best Dale Carnegie impression and sent the fan away happy.

Where Ted was emotional, John Muckler was analytical. I've always marveled at the way John's mind works. He's constantly thinking of new ways and techniques to improve the game. He's got it down to a science. His drills and his ability to break down tapes is incredible. When it comes to the technical part of the game, the man is a genius. He thinks, eats, and sleeps hockey. But for some strange reason, we always came out flat when John was behind our bench. Glen would take off to go boar hunting in Italy or fishing for great white sharks in Australia and he'd leave the team to John. Sure enough, the team would do nothing until Slats came riding back in on his white horse to save the day. For the longest time, we really gave Muck the raw end of the deal. We never meant to, but we always did. John has all the skills to be a successful head coach in the NHL, but he also has the perfect personality and attitude to play an assistant's role in Edmonton, though I'm sure there have been times it couldn't have been easy.

Nobody ever accused Slats of being shy. He likes the spotlight every bit as much as anybody else. I remember one of our annual open practices at Northlands Coliseum, where we'd get about 10,000 kids in the building to watch us work out. Slats came into the dressing room before practice to tell us that Muck had devised a bunch of brand-new special drills that fit together to make a real smooth-looking practice. Then he turned it over to John, who proceeded to explain all these new drills. Muck told us exactly what we'd do, how long we'd do each drill and the order we'd go through them. Once we got all that straight in our heads, we went out on the ice, expecting Muck to run the practice the way he always did. But Slats must have got excited about the crowd and wanted to be the ringleader, because he soon took over.

Slats banged his stick on the ice, telling us when to go as we'd burst back and forth between the bluelines. Then we followed that age-old bit with your basic "line up across the blueline for stationary shots." While all this standard stuff is going on, Muck's got nothing to do but stand off at the side, leaning on the boards.

So I skated over to him and said, "John, are all these new, intricate drills of yours running on schedule here?"

He just laughed and told me to screw off. He simply didn't care about the glory. John knows the game inside out, and I don't see how you'd get a better combination than Slats, Muck, and Ted Green.

You listened when Teddy talked because everybody in the room knew that he'd paid his dues. He was a hard-nosed guy. He'd been there, playing on those great Boston Bruins' teams with Bobby Orr and Phil Esposito. Muck was the great technician who knew exactly what had to be done. Teddy had done it. And Slats was the motivator.

He had various ways to motivate the team. He could be humorous. He could go into a frenzy. You just never knew which route he was going to take. He'd come into the dressing room when we were going through a bad spell and say, "I don't know what's the matter with you guys. Maybe you should all just relax and go out and get loaded." Sure enough, some of us would. Then the next morning Slats would bring us in and skate our asses off.

Sometimes when Slats started getting on different players,

it could get pretty funny. You had to bite your tongue hard.

"Wayne, you're too busy worrying about when the bank opens," he'd say to Gretz.

"Andy, all you care about is making pizza!" he'd shout at Glenn Anderson, who had an investment in a pizza store.

But you never really knew what to expect. He'd tell us one night that we'd better be prepared to bring our lunch pails to practice the next day. So we'd show up expecting a real tough skate and we'd end up playing minihockey, just fooling around. We'd think we were going to get skated right into the ice for an hour and a half. Then we'd get nothing.

Another time, we'd have a hard practice, then walk into the dressing room afterward to find the chairs all set up in front of the TV screen. Okay, we'd figure, we're going to go over the game films.

"Meeting in twenty minutes," Slats would say.

So we'd go have our showers and shaves, then get dressed and sit down to watch the films for an hour or so. Then he'd throw the curve ball.

"All right, we're going back out there," he would tell us.

Sure enough, we would. We'd all have to climb out of our street clothes, get all the hockey gear on again, and go for more practice.

He was always doing something different. Like threatening to put us on a schoolbus and take us all the way out to Vegreville for practice. That was only sixty miles. When things were going bad, Slats didn't want to talk to anybody. He'd come out of the hotel with a frown on his face, a cup of coffee in his hand, and his nose in the air. We called it his Million Dollar Strut. When things were going well, you could joke with him and have a great time. He could take the shots and give them out, too. But when he put the old strut on, it was no time for humor and he was unapproachable.

Sometimes, if the team hadn't been going right, he got miserable just to make us mad at him. "If you can't get mad at yourself, then get mad at me," he'd say. He could make that pretty easy when he wanted to. The man could go from one extreme to the other, but what made it all so effective was that we never knew where he was going to come from next.

A lot of guys I played with in Hartford and Toronto used

to tell me how much they despised Slats because of something he had said to them from the bench. His aim was to get under their skins and take them off their game, of course. But sometimes what Slats said or did motivated the other team and made them want to take out their frustrations with Sather on us. He's always in the thick of things. He almost seemed to enjoy getting into those confrontations with players from other teams and officials. He'd get a kick out of it. We'd hear him behind us, snickering away to himself. But that's the way he played the game. He was constantly bickering with people, trying to throw them off. That's something you just can't change. Especially when you enjoy it so much.

7

Sipping from the Cup

Y ou can have all the best players and you can have all the best coaches. But if you're going to win a Stanley Cup, then you'd better have the right chemistry. The Oilers had pails of it. We were creating tradition, though we didn't realize it at the time. We were just trying to win hockey games.

Some of the things we did to "help" us win had very little to do with hockey.

I don't think superstition's all that strange. But is it ever easy to get carried away.

We got to the point that every one of us had our own little routine. If you'd gone into our dressing room with a camera and videotaped what happened in there just before we went out onto the ice for the opening face-off, you'd see exactly the same routine from everybody every night. Same with the pregame warm-up. Gretz would move in and tap the goalie on the head. I always stood right in the crease by the goalie and when Paul Coffey came by, we'd hit gloves and he'd tap my shins with his stick before going on to the goalie. Jari Kurri was always the last guy to come in to the net.

It was like it had been choreographed. We'd take four months off in the summer, but the very first time the full team came together at training camp, that routine always picked right up again.

One summer, while I was busy doing nothing one day, I thought about that and started to worry. Geez, how am I supposed to remember all that stuff, I wondered. What happens if I miss my part? Do I throw everybody else off? For instance, if Paul went to tap my shins and I moved my leg, the first thing I'd have gotten was a dirty look. But training camp arrived and we got back onto the ice, and everything fell into place almost unconsciously.

Those crazy habits can start so innocently. I remember getting my knee taped only minutes before we went out to play the final game of the regular season. Just when our trainer, Peter Millar, finished wrapping my knee, Kevin Lowe was walking by, and Peter asked Kevin to pick up the scissors and cut the tape. We won the game that night. You guessed it. Every game from then on we had to give Kevin his little call and he'd have to come in and cut the last piece of tape on my knee. It didn't seem dumb. It seemed funny. We'd all stand around, with that one piece of tape dangling there, waiting for Kevin while he put on his skates or finished with something else. But nobody was going anywhere until he came in there and snipped the tape.

One of our superstitions when we were in the WHA days almost killed our left winger Brett Callighen. We had some unwritten rule that the whole team would pile off the bench and jump Brett whenever he scored a goal. We were supposed to be congratulating him. But we gave it to him pretty good. When he came out from the bottom of those piles, you could barely recognize him. His helmet would be almost hanging on one ear, his hair would be all messed, and his face would be beet red. He took so much punishment when he scored that it looked like he'd spent five minutes in a corner. Good job we never tried anything like that with Gretz. He scored so many goals, we'd have beaten him to death by Christmas in his first season.

But of all the superstitions we picked up along the way, if any one of them ever did amount to any good it had to be the Edmonton Oilers' "Wall of Fame." You've probably never heard of it because we never did advertise it much. But it was our American Express card. Come playoff time, we'd never leave home without it.

As we'd edged closer to contention for the Stanley Cup, we'd searched for inspiration from those who'd already been there. We started clipping pictures of famous players out of hockey magazines and sticking them on our dressing room wall. That famous picture of Bobby Orr, flying through the air a split second after he'd beaten Glenn Hall of St. Louis Blues in overtime to win the Stanley Cup for the Boston Bruins in 1970. Montreal Canadiens' classy Jean Beliveau, proudly lifting the Cup high over his head. It became our goal to have our own turn carrying that Cup. We'd look at the pictures and visualize ourselves in the photos. Soon those pictures became our own little traveling kit. We didn't bother with the routine during the regular season. But at playoff time those photos went everywhere with us. If we were just going down to Calgary for the night or if we were going to be away somewhere for four days, it didn't matter. We'd pack those pictures and find a place on the dressing room wall for them. I know a lot of people would just think, Look at that bunch of dumb jocks, carting their pictures around all over the continent. But those pictures were an inspiration, and damn it, we weren't going out on that ice until we had them set up properly on our wall. We kept adding to the collection. If we ever found a photo that could provide any sort of inspiration, bingo, it was on that wall. You'd look at a picture of a star from the past and visualize yourself in his position. You'd say to yourself, Hey, I can do that. I can stand up there like that, and someday, somebody else is going to have a picture of me on his wall and think the same thing.

The confidence helped and the confidence continued to grow. Even after the Islanders beat us four straight in '83, there wasn't any doubt in anybody's mind that we were going to get back into that final again the next year. We just had to go through the formalities of the regular season first. And what a year it was! We finished first in the league, going 57-18-5 for a winning percentage of .744. But that wasn't going to be even close to enough to keep us satisfied. We had come up with a lot of new things in Edmonton and had shown the hockey world an alternative way to play the game. Now we had to show them something else. We had to prove that the high-flying, offensive-minded Edmonton Oilers who had shattered all those scoring records could play the defensive style you need to win in the Stanley Cup playoffs. And there weren't many people around who were willing to bet five cents that we could.

To be brutally honest, I'm still not sure that even we thought we could do it before the first game of that series in the Nassau County Coliseum on Long Island. In all the other series leading up to the final with the defending champion Islanders, we'd been scoring tons of goals. There were only a handful of close contests. We had opened the playoffs that year with a 9-2 victory in Winnipeg, eventually sweeping the Jets three straight and outscoring them 18-7. Then we took a tough Smythe Division final series in seven games over Calgary, even though the Flames averaged four goals against us each game. And when we met Minnesota North Stars in the Campbell Conference final, we had the steamroller going strong again as we won it in four straight wide-open hockey games.

But then came the Islanders, the toughest defensive team in hockey, going for a fifth straight Stanley Cup to tie themselves on the all-time great list with the Montreal Canadiens. There was only one thing for us to do, only one way to win this thing. If we were going to beat the Islanders, we were going to have to play just like they did.

We'd studied them on tape and the coaches pointed out how we were going to have to come up the boards against them because they took away the middle of the ice so well. Prior to that final series we worked constantly on drills where we'd move the puck to the wingers. There was no sense trying to pass to the centre in the middle because the Islanders would always have that man picked up. But it left you other options. If you got stuck with nowhere to go up the boards, we tried to work it so we'd have a defenceman coming up late. Then we could throw the puck back to him and he could get it across the ice so we could bring it up the other side. Paul Coffey liked to come around from behind our net and go right up the boards.

The Islanders would put someone like big John Tonelli right in his path. Tonelli wasn't there to chase Coffey, just to meet him and force him to get rid of the puck. So we tried to get Coffey to utilize the middle more. We worked on those breakouts so much. But we also kept them simple. We had to. You couldn't get fancy against a team like the Islanders.

Everybody went out for game one a little more cautious than normal and thinking a lot more about defence than we'd ever done as a team before. Nobody wanted to make that crucial mistake. And the result was one of the finest hockey games any two teams are ever going to play anywhere, anytime. From the stands, you wouldn't have known there was any hesitation. It looked like everybody was going full out, all the time. But all the while, all night, people were thinking about their positions. Both teams. You were always thinking about when you could gamble or when you had to hold back. And everything just seemed to work.

It turned out to be a one-goal game and we got it. Wouldn't you know it, but that goal, which just might have been the most important one in Oilers' history, came from what first appeared to be a totally innocent play. No heroics by Gretzky. No end-to-end rush by Coffey. No wicked blast from Messier and no mad charge to the net by Glenn Anderson. Nothing like that. The puck seemed to be out of harm's way in the corner when Kevin McClelland just drifted in toward it through the face-off circle. All of a sudden the puck popped out onto his stick and he almost shoveled it into the net. All night long both teams had been coming so close, with great scoring chances, and we were beginning to wonder if it was ever going to go in. Grant Fuhr had been a rock in our net. Billy Smith was having a helluva night in goal for the Islanders. It had been fantastic, right from the end of the national anthems.

On my very first shift of the game, Slats had put me out with Gretz and Jari Kurri. We went down three-on-two and I'd thrown a pass cross-ice for Jari. I had led Jari with the pass by so much that it probably looked like I was trying to figure out everything from speed to angles to wind direction. What I was really doing was just firing it in the general direction of a blue sweater. It was like most of my passes — almost out of anyone's reach. But Jari stretched out and got the tip of his stick on the puck to deflect it right up near the corner of their net. He didn't miss scoring a goal by more than an inch or two. And when we had a chance like that, right off the start of the game, we thought it was going to be end-to-end all night with a big score. But the puck was only going to go into the net once all night. And even at that, when it finally did go in, we didn't even see it. Kevin's shot was right along the ice, and from our vantage point on the bench you couldn't see it through the crowd of players in front of he net. It even took Kevin a while to realize it was in, too. Of course, you weren't going to hear any cheers in that arena, so we couldn't count on the crowd to tip us off. Finally, finally, the goal light went on and it dawned on everybody. We'd put the puck in their net!

Two nights later, in the same building, we got ourselves trounced 6-1. We were too quick to think, Let's get this game over with and get out of here with a two-game lead. We weren't as patient and cautious as you have to be to win tight playoff hockey games. We thought we could grab another one and run before they realized what had happened. We didn't play the same way and they were connecting on everything. All of a sudden they got confident. Maybe too confident.

Bryan Trottier said something to one of the New York writers about how they had given us one game but then came back and toyed with us to win 6-1. You've got to understand that, at the time, a five-goal victory was the biggest differential ever in a Stanley Cup final history. But when we picked up the newspapers in the morning and read about Trottier saying the Islanders were back in the driver's seat, that was all the added incentive we ever needed.

We knew we had three games at home left, and we didn't waste any time. In the first game in our own building, we came right back and beat them by a five-goal differential, 7-2. Then we came back the next night and did it one more time, by exactly the same score. It was something the Islanders couldn't stop. They knew it was going to happen but couldn't do anything about it. I heard through the grapevine a while later that John Tonelli had said the Islanders were doubting themselves for the first time in years, wondering how they were going to stop us because we were just like a snowball, rolling downhill and gathering momentum as we went. Whatever the Islanders tried, we were one step ahead. And the more they doubted themselves, the more it got us going. And sure enough, in the fifth game, we rolled right over them again, 5-2, and the Stanley Cup was ours.

You never know where inspiration's going to come from when you need it most. When we'd lost that second game in New York, we'd gone into the dressing room and seemed to be almost waiting for someone to say something. I was never one to stand up and get the troops going. When things were real bad, Gretz wouldn't hesitate to speak his mind. Same with Mess. Mark's an emotional person and when he spoke, you listened. There was never any doubt that both of these guys were speaking from the heart. Everybody's different. But those two guys have that special trait. Surprisingly, it wasn't Wayne or Mark who got up to speak in the dressing room. It was Jaroslav Pouzar who came up with all the pep talk we needed. He told us all in that broken English of his how badly he really wanted to win. I think it surprised us all. He told us that no matter what we might think about the Stanley Cup not meaning as much to European hockey players as it does to guys who've grown up in Canada or the U.S., that idea was totally false. Pouzy told us that he wanted that Cup every bit as much as anybody else in our room, that he'd do anything to win it. That was a real inspirational thing for us, probably because it came from a quiet guy like Jaroslav who never really had much to say. He was getting on in his career, with only a year or two left, and he wanted to go back home to his native Czechoslovakia with a Stanley Cup championship to tell everybody back there about.

What was my little contribution to the cause? I'm glad you asked, because it was the biggest play of my career. Trouble is, nobody believes me.

We were only a couple of minutes into game four of that series, still in a scoreless tie, when the puck just came bouncing out over our blueline to centre ice right near our bench. I was going toward the boards to pick up the puck and even though I couldn't see Gretz because I was facing the other way, I knew he'd be long gone toward the Islanders' net. He was always doing that sort of thing. Don't ask me how he timed it. Don't ask me how he knew when to go and when to stay put. But he always seemed to know the perfect time to take off down the ice all by himself. He seemed to have a sixth sense about when the puck would come free to a teammate, who could then feed him a breakaway pass.

I figured he'd be headed right between the New York defencemen, so I just turned around and fired the puck as hard as I could without really aiming or looking. I thought I knew roughly where Gretz was heading. I'd throw it out there, and you never know, something good just might happen. I don't know if I've ever thrown a harder pass, but Gretz just stopped the puck like it was a feather. He cradled it, then he was gone. And even though Gretz was notorious for missing breakaways, I knew he wasn't going to miss that one. Sure enough, he didn't and we were away.

Ever since I've tried to convince everybody who will listen that was the greatest single play of my career. But none of my teammates ever believed me. They say I just panicked, as usual, and tried to ice the puck. I swore that I had an idea of the general direction Gretz was heading, but they still won't buy it. At that point, I was actually leading Gretz for career goals in a Stanley Cup final series. He hadn't scored against the Islanders the year before when we'd met them in the finals, but I'd managed to get one in that series. Then, in this year's finals, I'd scored the backbreaking seventh goal in our 7-2 win in game three. It wasn't until 12:08 of the second period in the fifth game of his second final series that Wayne Gretzky tied Dave Semenko for Stanley Cup final goals. He did leave me behind pretty quickly after that, though.

It took a long time for that Stanley Cup championship to sink in. What really threw it all off balance was the fans' reaction to Dave Lumley's empty-net goal with only thirteen seconds left in the third period of the fifth and final game. When Lummer put that puck into the Islanders' net, any glimmer of hope New York had for a comeback was gone. Our crowd knew that, too, and the celebration started. Unfortunately, a lot of them got carried away. They were trying to get onto the ice and littered it with all sorts of stuff. That took a lot away from the moment because we had a big delay while they cleared the ice, then we had some time left to play. Finally, those thirteen seconds ticked away and it was all over. I was out on the ice when the game ended, and I've got to confess that it didn't really hit me. I wasn't excited, for some reason. It was almost as if it hadn't been dramatic enough, that it should have been closer. Then we got into the dressing room and started playing the music we always played before we'd go on the ice, songs by the Thompson Twins and Aretha Franklin that were popular with a lot of guys and considered to be good luck charms. Finally, when that music began to play, it all started to sink in. It was an incredible high. But it would fade, then come back again, then fade and come back. It was like waves. Waves of joy.

The celebration seemed like it was never going to end. After the parade they had for us through those incredibly crowded streets downtown to the stage in front of Edmonton's City Hall, I was walking around with confetti in my hair for about three days. I lost all track of time. Completely. It was the best time of our lives. We had a little meeting the next morning in the dressing room with that Stanley Cup sitting there on our table-tennis board in the middle of the room. Slats was congratulating us on what we had accomplished, but we just couldn't wait to get out of there.

So as soon as Slats stopped talking, we scooped the Stanley Cup and headed for the bars. We were going to give anybody in Edmonton who was thirsty a sip out of that Cup, and I think most of them eventually did get a drink. Having won the Cup was fabulous, but just being around that trophy to see the effect it has on other people is incredible. It was amazing. Everything was in that Cup that day. If you think you've ever seen a shooter, you should have seen some of the B52s we mixed in the Stanley Cup.

What a fabulous feeling it was when Mark Messier, Kevin Lowe, and I drove out to St. Albert and took the Cup along with us. We had the sunroof open, and every once in a while we'd pop the Cup up through the hole in the roof and watch the reaction of the people in the cars around us. It was unbelievable. We'd have the horns honking and people in other cars smiling at us, clenching their fists, yelling, screaming, and applauding in midafternoon as they drove down the road.

We went to the Bruin Inn in St. Albert and there weren't many people in there at all. It was Mark Messier's neighborhood pub. So we put the Stanley Cup on one of the tables and played a little pool. Next thing you know, the few people who'd been in the place when we got there were all lined up behind one another at the pay phone, waiting to call their friends and tell them what was happening so they could come on down and see for themselves. We kept filling the Cup with beer and made sure everybody got a chance to have a drink from it.

Then it was my turn to take the Cup to my favorite restaurant, David's on Argyle. Everybody wanted a sip out of it. A beautiful afternoon. You've done the ultimate, and now you're taking the Stanley Cup around to share with your friends. If that isn't incredible, tell me what is.

I was especially proud to take it to my son's school. They sent a note home inviting me over to the school to talk with the kids about the Stanley Cup. So I brought the Cup home the night before and took it over to the school with me. I don't remember ever being any more proud and happy than that day. I only wish you could have been there with me to see the smiles on those faces.

Of course, we've all got our souvenirs. I have a photo of my youngest boy, Kelly, sitting in the Cup and his brother, Jason, standing there beside it. I also have one of my dad and me holding it up while we wore these big silly grins on our faces. That's a priceless picture. And there's one of Gretz and me afterward, at the team party following the game. That'll be one to keep for a lifetime.

Friends and family. They made this victory so much sweeter. My dad had made arrangements in advance to fly up to Edmonton for games three, four, and five of the final series. Then, when we took a 3-1 lead in games, my mom called.

"Are you going to win the series in five games?" she asked.

"Why five?" I asked her.

"Because if you're going to win for sure, then we'll drive up and watch," Mom said.

And they did. Mom drove up with my brothers Brad and Mark and their girlfriends. They drove from Winnipeg to Edmonton, purely on speculation and faith, hoping we'd wrap up the Cup at home where they could see us win the championship. I got everybody tickets and, well, it was just about perfect. The only one missing was my brother Brian, who couldn't make it to the game because he was overseas with the Canadian Armed Forces. But to have the rest of the family around made it so special. It added so much to the moment.

During the series I'd received telegrams from guys I'd played minor hockey with in Winnipeg, guys from East Kildonan. About six or seven of them were all getting together to watch the games. I could picture them down in their rumpus room, sipping their beers, watching me and cheering for us. I kept their telegram up on my stall and I'd read it every time before I went out on the ice. Great old friends: Randy Donkersloot, Rick McGillivray, George Young, Terry Mitchell, Rennie Balciunas, Darcey Zaporzan, Frank Redekopp. I would have been there for them, too, if it had been one of them who'd been playing for the Cup. I'd have been down in that rumpus room with all the buddies.

8

Playing with the Great One

Wayne Gretzky and I spent nine seasons together in Edmonton: one in the WHA and eight in the NHL. Talk about a prime ticket, I had one. For nine years, I had the best seat in the house to watch him every time he played hockey. I was front row center. People want to know how long it took for Gretz to impress me? That's never been a tough one to answer. One shift.

When it comes to hockey, nothing is impossible for him. After a couple of seasons, I lost count of the number of times I'd watched him do things that simply couldn't be done. At least, not by anyone else. And if you think watching him was fun, imagine how great it was to play on his line.

Through every one of those nine great years, whenever reporters came wandering over to my locker looking like they wanted an interview, I could figure the chances were about ninety-nine to one that the first question out of their mouths would be, "What's it like to be Wayne Gretzky's bodyguard?" It was the stock question of all stock questions.

And there was a stock answer.

I wasn't anybody's personal bodyguard. I was a member of the Edmonton Oilers hockey club. And if anybody on my team needed help, I was there to help him. If I see a friend of mine, on or off the ice, being taken advantage of, then I'll step in and stop it. My job wasn't to fight someone else's battles for him. Gretz fought his battles on the scoreboard, where he was the undisputed heavyweight champion of the world. Me? I just liked to make sure that nobody tried to take any sort of unfair advantage.

When Gretz first came to Edmonton, nobody really knew how special he was. He'd only played a few games for the Indianapolis Racers and nobody knew much about him.

I could remember seeing something about him on "Hockey Night in Canada." They had pictures of this little kid skating around while his dad stood watching. He only looked about four years old, but he was an incredible skater for his age, a real phenomenon. Aside from that one little bit on TV, I didn't know anything about him. I sure didn't realize that in the seventeen-year-old kid we had a superstar on our hands.

When Gretz, Eddie Mio, and Peter Driscoll all came to Edmonton in that one deal, I thought Driscoll was the most important guy. As far as management was concerned, Gretz was for the future. I couldn't see that far ahead. And I didn't know much about Eddie, so I had no idea if he'd help us in goal.

I'd played against Peter and I knew what he was like: a big, strong, aggressive left winger with a good shot. It was a relief to have him because he could play tough and fight and was going to take a little pressure off me.

I guess you could say there's a little difference between myself and Gretz. He lives in Los Angeles, I live in Edmonton. He has a daughter. I have two sons. Other than that, the similarities are rather remarkable.

Ron Chipperfield and I were talking about hockey injuries one day, when I told him that some tests the Oilers ran showed that Gretz and I had roughly the same level of flexibility, which really wasn't much compared with all the other guys on the team.

"Isn't that strange?" I asked Ron. "You're supposed to be susceptible to injuries if you aren't flexible. Yet Gretz and I are the least flexible guys on the team and neither of us has ever had a major injury."

"That's no mystery," Chipper replied. "It's just common sense. One they can't hit and one they won't."

And there's one of the big secrets to the successful life of number 99. You can't hit him. He's got built-in radar. In the early days, there were all sorts of guys around who wouldn't have hesitated if they got the chance to take off his head, but they never got the chance. People couldn't cheap-shot Gretz because he never lost track of where everybody else was out there. Well, hardly ever. During all the years we were both Oilers, I only saw him get nailed with his head down once. It happened during our second NHL season in a game against the Toronto Maple Leafs. Gretz was coming out across our blueline when Bill McCreary caught him with his head down and laid a real good, clean check onto him. Gretz went down like he'd been shot and stayed there for a long time. McCreary only played twelve NHL games that year but he sure made his mark that night. And he left it on Gretz. But that's it and that's all. Aside from that one shot, I never saw Gretz get leveled in nine seasons. He's a magician.

To play on his line meant that my name went into the pool all the players had going. We'd always be fooling around, looking for ways to occupy our time. Gretz had Jari Kurri on his right wing for all those years, and the two of them were poetry in motion. There were nights when you'd have thought they shared the same brain. But on Wayne's left side you'd get the player of the week. Or the night. Or maybe just the first period. Wayne had more left wingers than Gorbachev, so somebody came up with a Gretzky Left Winger Pool. We'd put numbers in a hat, then draw for how many shifts the new winger was going to last. The lower the number you drew — meaning the fewer shifts it would take before Slats switched wingers again — the better chance you had of winning the money.

It did so much for your confidence to play with Wayne. You knew you were going to get a couple of chances to score. With me, the puck didn't necessarily have to go in to keep me happy. Just being close and having the opportunity was sometimes good enough. At least you knew you'd been in position. When you go for games at a stretch without ever getting a shot on net and playing all night between the bluelines, it can really get frustrating.

But then there would come that day when you'd walk into

the dressing room the day after we'd lost a game. The lines would be changed and when I looked at the board, there it was up at the top: 27, 99, 17. Me, Gretz, and Jari.

You'd get to wear that almighty red sweater during practice. That's when I had to make sure I was really ready, because I knew I'd be playing a lot. A regular shift plus the power plays. And all I had to do was go up and down my wing, knowing that Gretz was going to find my stick somehow.

He was good for three or four good scoring opportunities on any night I ever played on his line. That's a lot of opportunities. And they were automatic. Even when he was off his game, which wasn't often, you were going to get a sniff there somewhere.

All you had to do with Gretz was let him get that puck over the blueline first, then come late. Everybody used to give him the gears about having trouble with breakaways. Hell, I never had one where I had to worry about some guy chasing me as I went toward the other net. Nobody was going to trip me from behind and give our team a penalty shot. Not when they knew that if they left me alone and let me go, I'd probably just shoot the puck into the corner, anyway.

Being late always was my specialty. I've smoked up to a pack of cigarettes a day for years; nobody ever had to tell me twice to be late coming up the ice. When I first went to Edmonton, a lot of guys on the team smoked. Three or four of us even used to sneak a cigarette in the dressing room between periods, ridiculous though it seems now. We'd go into the bathroom and have a glass of Gatorade while we fired up our smokes. Some nights, especially when I was just sitting on the bench and not playing, that between-period smoke break was something to look forward to.

However, there was one day when Wayne and I were in pretty well the same physical condition. We were both wrecked. And we couldn't have picked a worse time.

Up to the end of my second year of pro hockey, I'd never heard of a fitness test. Then, all of a sudden, technology stepped in and the coaches had what could be called a stroke of genius.

We had come to the end of our final year in the WHA. It

had been Wayne's rookie season and he had finished with forty-six goals, three with Indianapolis Racers and forty-three for us. He'd given it his best shot. We all had. And when it ended just short of the championship, we all had ourselves a small party that only lasted about seventy-two hours.

But believe it or not, three days after we'd been knocked out of the playoffs, the coaches called us all in for fitness tests! I think one of them probably just stumbled on to this and said, "Hey, there's still a few guys wandering around town. Let's give this a try." Or maybe they wanted to work the bugs out before they used the tests again at training camp in the fall. It was probably one of Dave Dryden's bright ideas. He was always hanging around the University of Alberta looking for something new.

Well, you should have seen us going through the running and cycling and everything after we'd been partying for a few days. Gretz threw up. Guys were groaning all over the place. And I almost drowned in the dunk tank.

I tried to get an appointment as late in the morning as possible so I'd have at least a little rest under my belt. And I must have had a solid two hours' sleep before I showed up for my eleven o'clock appointment. Things were going okay for a while. Then they decided to test me for body fat. Now anytime anyone had ever done that before they'd used calipers. But this time they decided they'd use the dunk tank.

So there I am, sitting on this metal bar above the tank, half asleep and the other half hung over while they explained what they were going to do. All of a sudden, they hit the switch and I dropped into the tank without having a chance to catch a breath of air. They checked this dial and that dial, writing down this and noting that. They were all gawking at Gretz while I was down in the bottom of this damned tank, banging on the walls and trying to get someone's attention. I don't know how many gallons I swallowed before they hoisted me out.

From then on, I was ready for these tests. I had to be. I ran a lot and lifted weights. But mostly I just skated myself into shape long before training camp opened. In the early years of my career I'd skate with the Wheat King juniors in Brandon. Later on in Edmonton a bunch of us would rent ice and work out. But I had to be ready.

Which goaltender was toughest on me? Every one of them. And I had just as much trouble with the goal posts. Realistically, I can never think of a particular instance when I felt I was robbed by a goaltender — I always felt I was stealing from them whenever I scored. I played in front of the net a lot, so I got credit for scoring goals that bounced in off my ribs or my rear end. The odd one even went in off my stick.

My hands were not quite as soft as Wayne's. Then again, he didn't have to bang his on all those helmets.

Things tended to get a little scary when I was standing in front of the net and someone put the puck on my stick. You never knew what was going to happen next or who was going to get hurt. Let me try to tuck it in the top corner and I was just as likely to take out someone coming down the stairs in the stands with a bag of popcorn.

Where Gretz didn't have the touch was in practice. He could drive you crazy. He was absolutely the worst guy you'd want to have to play on a line with during practice.

I never did figure out if Gretz was doing it to me on purpose. He was able to do so many things with the puck without showing any effort that you could never tell what was an accident and what was intentional. We had a three-on-two drill during which Gretz would start by going around the back of the net and throwing a pass up to me on the wing. In a game, that pass was going to be laid on your stick perfectly, with whatever weight behind it that you'd told Wayne you wanted. Perfect weight and perfect lead. Every time. But not in practice. He'd flip the puck and it would come bouncing across the ice at me. I'd be batting away, trying to knock the thing down and get the return pass back to him when I'd look up and see him skating by, laughing at me. He was not a practice player. He had a great time at practice and when he had to be serious, he would be. But at almost every workout, whenever a player made a mistake, no matter how serious it was, every other player would be all over the guy. Invariably, Gretz would get more criticism from the nineteen other guys than he'd get if they filled the Coliseum with fans for practice.

There never was any doubt who the leader was. He didn't make a habit of giving speeches in the room, but Wayne would tell us what was on his mind when he felt the time was right. Gretz, Mess, or Kevin would usually be the ones to call a team meeting. Many times the coaches would have their say at the end of a practice, and then we players would have a meeting of our own to discuss some things. It never got down to specifics about individuals during the players' meetings. It was always more of a "support your teammate" or "we've gotta work together" message. We had so much fun winning that we really missed it when we didn't have that country club atmosphere in our dressing room. When we had the coaches, fans, and media on our backs, we realized that the only thing we could do about it was to work harder and get back to basics. And nobody worked harder than Gretz. He led by example.

Mario Lemieux of the Pittsburgh Penguins might be one of the many players who learned from the way Gretz went about his job. For a long time, I really didn't have much respect for Lemieux. Whenever we played Pittsburgh, Gretz would always seem to show Lemieux up. Reporters would try to talk to him after the game and he'd be long gone. But Gretz was always there to answer the questions, even if he'd played a lousy game, which wasn't very often. And even if we'd lost the game, which wasn't very often, either. Gretz wanted to get out of that dressing room, just like the rest of us. When you win, you want to get out of there and celebrate. When you lose, you want to get out even faster. But he always had to stay to answer the questions. Wayne would be there to speak with the reporters while Lemieux dodged the media bullets.

We'd get selfish, especially on the road where we'd all have to wait for him. We'd be out on the bus waiting for Wayne to wrap up the interviews and it was only natural to complain. I even caught myself at it once, thinking, C'mon Gretz, hurry up. How stupid was that? We'd forget about the burden he carried and think we were hard done by because our bus got held up for a little while. There was Gretz, taking all the shots, and there we were bitching about having to wait ten minutes for the Franchise.

The things he did had to rub off. I'm convinced the 1987 Canada Cup had a lot to do with the change and growth of Mario Lemieux into a bona fide superstar. He got to play with the best, Wayne Gretzky, and it's amazing what can happen in the dressing room when you associate with winners.

Shortly after that Canada Cup I remember watching a game on TV when Lemieux dragged two opposition guys with him all the way from center ice. He didn't even seem to think about them as they hooked and hacked at him. He just went on in and scored. A lot of guys would have stopped. A year or two before that Canada Cup series, Lemieux might have quit, too. But he's got that competitive fire now, and I'm convinced it was lit when he shared the Team Canada dressing room with Gretz during that series against the Soviet Union.

Gretz could give you an assist without ever passing you the puck. I'm pretty sure I got one of those after an incident in Boston one year. We'd had a pretty good practice and there didn't seem to be any storm clouds brewing on our horizon, when all of a sudden Slats called a team meeting.

"David, I don't know what's the matter with you," he said to me. "I don't think you care anymore. I think you're just content sitting in the back of the bus telling jokes. I don't know if you even want to play anymore."

He went up one side of me and down the other about my attitude. Then, a couple of days later in New York, we were having a pregame meal when Slats stood up to talk.

"Semenk, how long have we been together?" he said.

"I dunno, Slats," I said. "About nine years, I think."

"That's right, nine years," Sather says. "You've been here as long as I've been here. I want all you other guys to think about that for a minute. Do you know why Semenk's been here that long? Because of his attitude, that's why. Sometimes he wasn't playing much but he'd never complain. He never went whining to the press about ice time, never gave it the play-me-or-trade-me crap or moped around the dressing room. A lot of you guys are selfish if things aren't going right for you. We don't have room for that on this team. Semenk's been here this long and hasn't ever complained about anything."

What in the hell was that all about? Who changed his tune? It was the total reverse of the lecture I'd received in front of everybody just a couple of days before. Gretz must have said something to him.

Perhaps he did. Perhaps not. But he did have to say the one word to the Oilers that I never thought I'd hear through his lips: goodbye.

My reaction was total disbelief. I was lying in bed reading the paper and came across an article saying the Montreal *Gazette* claimed that the deal was almost done, Wayne Gretzky was going to be traded. Naturally, I didn't believe it. I didn't believe it was possible when I played on the same team with Wayne. I didn't believe it possible when I played in Hartford and Toronto. And I still didn't believe it could happen now that I was out of hockey. But just then the phone rang and one of the guys from a local TV station was calling. He said the trade was a 99.9 percent certainty and that he'd like to bring a camera over and get my reaction.

"Sorry, I'm busy," I told him, even though I wasn't. They were flashing a message across the bottom of the television screen. Stay tuned, a live press conference was going to follow at 3:00 p.m. That did it. I wasn't going anywhere until I got all the details. Like everybody else in Edmonton that day, I was glued to the screen.

They put the cameras on Pocklington who threw everyone a curve ball: *Wayne had asked to be traded.* I couldn't figure out what the hell was going on. We'd said for years that if Pocklington ever tried to trade Gretz, they'd burn down the Coliseum. Peter would have to leave town. He wouldn't trade him, would he? He couldn't. Gretz meant so much to everybody. But now Peter was saying it was Wayne who had asked for the trade.

I believed it. For at least two minutes, maybe three, I believed it. Then I realized it was a lot easier for Gretz to take the heat and that's the game they were playing.

If I'd still been with the Oilers organization when Gretz was traded — and hadn't gone with him to L.A. as Marty

McSorley did — I'd have been bothered to no end. That's like taking money out of someone's pocket. You could sit on the Edmonton bench and know you were in trouble, but also know that sooner or later, Gretz was going to do something about it. There was always a light at the end of the tunnel when he was there. I can only imagine how much it must have hurt to have that taken away.

From Pocklington's side, there was business to consider. Who came out ahead? Well, Wayne certainly won round one when he had such a great year with the Kings and they beat the Oilers in the 1989 Smythe Division semifinal. But down the road Edmonton has a lot of draft choices it obtained in that trade and you never know what's going to happen in the next couple of years. You build a winner through the draft. That's a proven fact. You can try the quick fix, but it doesn't always work. We'll have to be patient and wait a few seasons to find out who really got the better of the deal, though. It's too early to judge now. Besides, there's still so much emotion involved because of the way the people of Edmonton loved Wayne.

The more I sat there thinking about the trade, the more one thought kept coming back to me. All of a sudden, I didn't feel so bad about having been traded before. I'd thought that I was one of the Untouchables. But when the true one gets shipped off, it really sinks in: nothing lasts forever.

We had our moments, though. We shared something real special through all the years with those Edmonton teams. And while I never did agree with being thought of as Wayne Gretzky's bodyguard, I'll be the first one to admit that it never hurt me at all. I got a lot of name recognition by being associated with Wayne. If I hadn't played on the same team for nine seasons, I wonder how many people would have heard of Dave Semenko.

So let me tell you a little secret. It almost didn't happen. I was almost involved in the deal that brought Gretz to Edmonton in the first place. It scares me just to think about it.

Pocklington and Nelson Skalbania, who owned the Racers and Wayne's personal services contract, had agreed to a deal that would send me and some money to Indianapolis. From there, I was going to be traded to Minnesota. I was having lunch in Champ's Restaurant at the Northlands Coliseum when Bob Freeman, one of the first and finest friends I'd made when I moved to Edmonton, came walking over to my table. Slats had sent him. Bob told the waitress he'd pick up my check and asked me to come with him to the Oilers' office right away. He was dead serious and wouldn't say a word. He wouldn't tell me a thing about what was going on. We just sat outside the coach's office, waiting. After a couple of hours, Slats stuck his head out of the office and told me to go home. Only later did I find out that while I was out there waiting, he was on the phone convincing Peter to stop the trade.

And while I'm telling secrets, let me drop another one on you. Contrary to anything Peter Pocklington might ever have said, Wayne Gretzky doesn't need acting lessons. Paul Baxter, who's gone on to coaching now, knows all about that.

Baxter was playing for the Penguins when we came into Pittsburgh one night. What set it off is long forgotten, but he and Gretz had something going. Finally, Baxter struck Gretz, who immediately hit the ice as though he'd been shot.

What a scene that was! The trainers were called out onto the ice. The paramedics were on standby. Somebody brought a stretcher out.

"You all right, Wayne? Are you all right?" our trainer kept asking him.

"I'm fine," Wayne whispered. "How's the crowd taking it?"

After Gretz had done his little thing, Baxter kept threatening Wayne. Every time he skated past our bench, he'd say something to Gretz. Finally he skated over to our bench at the middle of the second period, waved his stick in Wayne's face, and said, "Hey, Gretzky, I'm gonna cut your eyes out."

I stood up so I could get a little more leverage and threw the best right I could at Baxter. I hadn't seen anything behind him, but it turned out that Dave Lumley had seen him waving his stick at our bench, so he was running at Baxter from the middle of the ice. Lumley nailed him real good from one side just as I was punching him from the other, and it was good night, Paul.

It was good night, Dave, too. That's the shortest game I

never played. I hadn't been on the ice for the first thirty minutes and now, after dropping Baxter from the bench, I was given a game misconduct and sent to the dressing room for the rest of the game.

The longest stretch I ever spent on Gretzky's line was during the 1984 playoffs. I'd started out on a line with Ken Linseman and Willy Lindstrom during the first playoff series against Winnipeg. Then in the next series, against Calgary, Slats put me out with Gretz and Jari. I was with them through that series, the next one against Minnesota North Stars and the Stanley Cup final against the Islanders. In one of those games against Minnesota, I was a plus six. All I'd done during the entire game was stand in front of the net. The defencemen weren't moving me and I was bugging the goaltender on almost every shot that came his way. Talk about fun!

But then it was always fun out on the ice when Gretz was around. You never knew what was going to happen next. Sometimes it would be a miracle, like the time I got four points in the last ten minutes of a game in Quebec. We were down by three goals when I took a cross-checking penalty on Brent Ashton. Every time I went to the penalty box, I looked on the bright side. I always dreamed that this time, maybe, I'd be able to come sneaking out of there at the end of the penalty, grab a pass or a loose puck, and get myself a breakaway. And I'll be damned if it didn't finally happen. I came out, walked into a breakaway, and scored a goal.

Glen then put me back out with Gretz and Glenn Anderson. There's a play we used for face-offs in the opposition end. Our centreman would try to draw the puck back to the point and the winger who'd been lined up against their defenceman on the hash marks in the slot would drift away from the defenceman. Then he could take the pass from the point and quickly let it go at the net. Everything went fine until the puck came to me from the point and I had to one-time it. I just barely hit the puck and it skipped all the way to the net. I think the goalie must have gotten dizzy watching the puck bounce in toward him, because Anderson ended up with the rebound and scored on him.

On the next sequence of plays, I passed the puck to Gretz

and went for the net. Wayne found Andy and he put it in the corner of the net. Moments later, Charlie Huddy got the puck to me behind the net and I threw it out front to Andy, who scored the winning goal. Four points in ten minutes.

At that time we'd been trying out some new equipment. We'd had a lot of shoulder injuries for some reason or another, and we were trying Cooper shoulder pads that were more like football gear than hockey equipment. They were a real awkward fit compared with anything we were used to.

The morning after that game with Quebec I ran into Slats at the airport and told him he'd better do something about these new pads.

"I can't be wearing these things," I told him. "They're giving me a rash under my arms from raising my hands up in the air after I score all these goals."

I'm surprised Gretz didn't wear his arms out raising them after every goal he scored. But I'm sure glad he didn't because I wouldn't have wound up with a brand-new Dodge in my driveway after the NHL all-star game at Edmonton in 1989.

I didn't hear anything about this car until the next morning when I walked into the real estate office where I work and people started saying things I didn't understand.

"Dave, when are you going to give us a ride in your new car?" everybody asked.

I was beginning to wonder whether someone had slipped something into the office coffeepot when someone handed me a newspaper and said, "Read this! It says right here that Gretzky is giving you the car he won for being named Most Valuable Player in the game last night."

This can't be happening, I thought. And even if it was, I didn't know what I was supposed to do about it. I didn't know who to contact. All kinds of media guys were calling to ask me about this and I didn't know what to tell them. I sure wasn't going to phone every automobile dealer in town and ask them if they had a car there for me. I didn't want to come across as sounding too anxious or too greedy. I wanted at least to seem to be cool about it. Finally, I got through to Wayne's manager, Mike Barnett, who told me who I should contact.

I remember telling Wayne that when a couple of days went

by without me hearing anything from the Chrysler people, I was convinced they had the car in the shop and were stripping it down. I figured when they found out Gretz was giving the car to me, they were ripping every option out of it. Wayne would have got everything specially made, but by the time they rolled it out for me, all that would be left was a couple of tires and a steering wheel. It sure didn't work out that way, though. They let me load it to the hilt.

Ironically, the car has a black exterior. I wanted a burgundy interior, but the only colors available on that model were beige and silver. So I ordered silver. And it wasn't until a week later I realized I'd be getting a car with L.A. Kings' colors. Now, if I can only get license plates that say MVP 27 I can have a lot of fun.

I know Wayne doesn't do it on purpose. But for nine years of my career, I answered the same question: "What is Wayne Gretzky really like?" I got it everywhere I went. Then it became "What about that trade?" And I had to answer all the people who wanted to know my feelings about Wayne's trade to Los Angeles. Then when that died down, all of a sudden Wayne gives me a car. Now everybody wanted to know my reaction to that.

I'm convinced the guy is determined to have me talking about him for the rest of my life. Just when I think it's safe to go out of the house, Gretz finds a new angle.

9

The Battle of Alberta

I cannot imagine ever putting on a Calgary Flames jersey. Shoot me first, thanks. The Edmonton-Calgary rivalry is alive and thriving. I couldn't see anybody who'd played for a while with that key group we had together for five or six years in Edmonton going down to Calgary and playing the way he had while he was an Oiler.

It took a while for what they now call the Battle of Alberta to get into the players' blood. A lot longer than it did for the fans, that's for sure. They showed up with hate in their eyes from day one.

I never had any problem going out in Calgary. None of us did. We'd usually go to one of the clubs along what they call Electric Avenue and were never bothered. The people were willing to leave the game at the rink.

Get them in Olympic Saddledome and you've got a different story. That came home to me when I injured my knee down there. I had my skate blade caught in a rut when Paul Baxter hit me. My right knee had popped and I had to get off the ice as quickly as possible. They were enjoying it too much — actually cheering! So I got up on my own and half-limped and half-skated out of there. I wasn't going to crawl to the bench. I wasn't going to give the crowd that satisfaction. If you wore an Edmonton uniform, the last thing you wanted was a bunch of Calgarians hooting at you.

Almost everybody on our team had played a couple of seasons against the Flames when they were still based in Atlanta. So for the players, for a year or so after the Atlanta franchise was shifted to Calgary, it was hard to get all caught up in any special feeling. These were the same old guys. They wore red-and-white uniforms. We almost always won. No big deal.

But once the Flames became established with a Calgary identity, things got real testy. The media and the fans in both cities built the rivalry up to the point that every game between the two teams was a major event.

There was almost a script. I'd be fighting Tim Hunter and Don Jackson would fight Jim Peplinski. It was automatic.

There were rare times during the season when I'd look at the game coming up and think, Great! Their fighter's out with an injury or suspension, so maybe I can go out there and play hockey tonight.

Not against Calgary, though. You knew what was going to happen. It was only a matter of time. We played a lot of back-to-back games with them. If something didn't happen the first night, it was sure to break out during the second.

It never really seemed to matter who was leading or losing, who won or lost. It was a matter of match-ups. When you went into a game and knew it was 99.9 percent certain before they dropped a puck that you were going to have to fight a particular guy, nothing else mattered. Not the schedule. Not the standings. You and whoever the other guy was that night would just watch each other, knowing that sooner or later something was going to happen. The puck could be in your corner but you weren't watching it. You were looking for that other player, making sure he didn't sneak up on you.

It never came down to Tim Hunter and me developing some sort of mutual respect for each other. Somehow, we were just expected to fight. He'd do something to one of our players or I'd do something to one of theirs and away we'd go.

I wasn't afraid of Hunter and he wasn't afraid of me. There was never any big winner in our fights. Most of the time we came away with a draw and neither of us was going to come flying out of that box as soon as our penalties had expired to do it again. We'd have our clash, then it would be over with.

And it was usually enough that each of us skated away thinking he'd won.

Hunter is very strong. He keeps himself in tremendous physical condition, so he was probably a lot stronger than me. He knew I'd only use my right hand and he'd take some punches to get into a position where he could grab hold of my right arm and force me to trade lefts with him. His left-handed punches were stronger than mine, but they weren't very fast and were pretty easy to duck. I could see them coming for days.

Hunter and I did have some long drawn-out affairs. I think the only decent punch I ever landed on him came during a game in Calgary one night when I managed to get away from a linesman somehow. We'd gone at it for a while when the linesmen came in to break up the fight and tied both of us up. They were sandwiched between us. But there was this little space between them and I could see Hunter's face about one foot in front of mine. He was yapping away at me. All of a sudden, just for an instant, the linesmen let go of my right arm. Believe me, things like that don't happen very often. When those guys get hold of you, it's usually a death grip. Once they move in, you might as well forget trying to throw any more punches because you aren't going to get away from them too often. But here was my golden opportunity. Having that hand freed was like a gift from God. So I let go and brought it in, straight over the top. To this day I don't know how I missed Hunter's nose. But I got him flush in the middle of his forehead, and he went straight over backward.

I remember Peplinski more for his mouth than his fists. I met him a couple of times at the NHL slowpitch tournament. But the only time I ever remember talking to him was while I was beating up one of his teammates, Jamie Macoun.

Macoun didn't play tough. He was a rushing, aggressive defenceman. I fought him once or twice and it never amounted to much. Once, in the Corrall, I got out of my straitjacket. I saw Paul Coffey wrestling with one Flame, so I skated over and suckered the Calgary player. All of a sudden, Coffey had to hold the guy up. Then I got into it with Macoun and mopped up there pretty quick, too.

Dave Lumley had suckered Peplinski, who was bleeding

all over the place right beside me. I had hold of Macoun at the time. Our little tussle was all over and done, so I looked over at Peplinski and said something sarcastic.

"I'm all right," Peplinski told me, "it's just a nosebleed."

So I looked back at Macoun, let go of the front of his sweater and threw three or four more good punches. Boom, boom, boom, boom. I got him good with every one, then grabbed on to his sweater again.

"What the hell is that supposed to be?" Peplinski yelled at me.

"Why, Jim, don't you know?" I said. "That's called a flurry."

I always had a lot of respect for another Flame, Lanny McDonald, both as a human being and a hockey player. But I lost it all in the seventh game of our 1984 Smythe Division championship playoffs.

The game was all wrapped up and Calgary was history. We were up 7-4, and it was the last shift of the game when he tried to take my knees out. McDonald came in to check me very low. Another guy who used to play for Calgary, Hilliard Graves, used to do the same thing. In fact, Graves got quite a reputation as a career-wrecker. Your knees can really get screwed up by those submarine shots. You're especially vulnerable to them when you get a little careless and watch the puck after you've passed instead of watching out for someone coming at you. And I sure didn't expect it on this night. There were only twenty seconds left in the game, and here comes McDonald, deliberately going after my knees. I'm only lucky he didn't do some serious damage. To my mind, he tried to hurt me. I didn't get a chance to say anything to him about it at the time. I had a better revenge. I'd half-dodged him, and we both were sprawled on the ice as we watched that clock tick off the final seconds of Calgary's hockey season. I enjoyed that moment a little more than McDonald did.

I don't care about all the stuff he might do for charities. I'm never going to forget that he deliberately went at my knees when the game was as good as over.

But if we're going to talk about respect, or lack of it, then I've got to save space for Doug Risebrough. He's one of

Calgary's assistant coaches now, but I remember him more for a stunt he pulled while he was their captain.

I've never met Risebrough away from the ice. I don't think I ever met him on it, either. When I think back to eleven years of pro hockey, it's amazing the number of players on different teams who were never on the same ice surface at the same time I was. So there was no friction for me personally with Risebrough, because I never played against him. But I sure heard him. He might have had the foulest mouth in the NHL. That's fine. It's a free country. Risebrough can say whatever he wants to say. But he came to Calgary from the Montreal Canadiens organization, and I think he forgot his roots somewhere on the trip west.

In Montreal, if a player ever walked into the Canadiens' dressing room and threw his sweater on the floor, he'd answer to Jean Beliveau or Guy Lafleur or someone else in a long, long line of Montreal stars and captains. That sweater was sacred, not some dishrag. In a game against Risebrough and the Flames, one of our guys, Marty McSorley, had his sweater pulled right off him. Somehow Risebrough got hold of Marty's sweater in the penalty box and did a dance on it, cutting it to ribbons with his skates.

It was what the drunkest fan in the highest row might do to another team's sweater. It sure wasn't anything I'd ever have expected from a professional hockey player who'd been around as long as Risebrough and had played for Stanley Cup champions. If it had been some freshman at the University of Calgary putting an Oiler's sweater on a stick then dousing it with gas, lighting it, and marching around the campus, well, that's one thing. But for a veteran like Risebrough? I hope he's proud to have that one on his track record.

One ex-Flame who lost my respect was Neil Sheehy. I have no use for a tough guy who's supposed to be a fighter falling on the ice and turning turtle to draw a penalty. I've seen Sheehy in games that were already decided try to do things like that to draw a penalty. And with a cockiness that was so infuriating that you'd want to leap over the boards and fight him.

He knew it, of course, and he played it to the hilt. I'll give him credit for one thing: he could get under your skin further and faster than anybody I ever played against. He almost drove us up the wall in the 1986 playoffs, when Calgary beat us in the Smythe Division final.

The way that series went was so frustrating for Marty McSorley, Kevin McClelland, and me. Slats said the Flames were going after Gretz so we should retaliate and go after their smaller guys like Hakan Loob — stick them with an elbow, just to see how they liked it.

But Marty, Kevin, and I didn't play that way. We'd all go after the tough guys — no problem. We were geared that way. But we weren't going to pound on some small guys.

The Flames did, though, and it worked. Paul Coffey has a short fuse and so does Gretz. Sheehy would give Coffey a shove in the face, and all of a sudden Paul would snap. Get him into a fight, and he's completely off his game.

Sheehy would use the same sort of tactics to get to Gretz, and it would work just as well. He would give Gretz a little shove after the whistle or chirp at him, something cheap to try to antagonize Wayne.

He frustrated Gretz, but he frustrated me even more because I couldn't get at the guy. He wouldn't fight. He'd shove and stick and antagonize until one of our smaller guys lost it and tried to get into it with one of their heavies. All of a sudden, the armed forces would be called out off our bench. Marty, Kevin, or I would go out there to fight this guy, and after we'd thrown one punch, Sheehy would be on his hands and knees on the ice covering his head with his arms. And we'd be in the penalty box.

We didn't fight fire with fire. If we didn't care about our egos and reputations, it would have been very easy for us to go after their small stars. A glove in the face or a stick in the back of the legs gets a message home real quick. But we didn't have that mentality on our team. We were tough guys and were only going to go after tough guys.

Obviously, we should have done something differently. They won the series, not us.

10

A Lesson from the Islanders

In all the time I played hockey, I never enjoyed the game any more than when we met the New York Islanders. That was good hockey. It was hard. Lots of hitting, but no cheap shots. Once, early on, I hit Brent Sutter. He was one of the Islanders' smaller players at five foot eleven and 175 pounds, but he was rugged like the rest of his family and played the game hard. But after our collision, Bobby Nystrom, who was about six foot one and 200 pounds, came skating over to me.

"Let's just play the game," Nystrom said. "You can run at me as hard as you want, but let's let those other guys play."

That was fine by me. I would not go out of my way to get at one of their stars. I wasn't going to go after Mike Bossy. What would that prove? It was nice to play against a Nystrom or a Clark Gillies. They were good and tough. They were honest hockey players. I always thought Gillies was the ultimate. He was big and strong. When he fought he got the job done, and he didn't have to do it very often. I wanted to be like that. He'd play on the all-star team, get his thirty goals a year, and nobody pushed him around. You can't get a better combination than that in a hockey player. And I wasn't the only one. Coaches drooled over guys who could play the offensive game and also play tough, aggressive hockey. And that's the style we'd play against the Islanders during my days with the Oilers. Of course, things had changed considerably by the time I was with Hartford and then Toronto. Not only were the Whalers and Maple Leafs drastically different teams than the Oilers, but by that time, the Islanders had changed, too, and many of the bigger and better players from their dynasty days had either retired or had moved to other teams.

But what a treat it was to play New York during the early '80s. I could go up and down my wing, and every once in a while there'd be a little clash when we went for the puck. It was like a dream come true to play them in the Stanley Cup finals in 1983 and 1984. I didn't have to fight. I could go out and play hockey the way it should be played.

Only one thing about playing the Islanders really turned me off: their goaltender and renowned dirty player, Billy Smith. One day, right out of the blue, Slats became concerned about my safety, for some reason. We were due to play the Islanders, and Slats wanted me standing in front of their net, but he figured I'd need some extra protection, since Smitty was going to be standing behind me with the ax he called a goalie stick. Slats said he'd like me to wear ankle guards. Gee, isn't that nice, I thought. Smitty's going to try to break my ankle. Won't this be fun. I'll be in the hospital, watching the games on TV while my teammates try to win the Stanley Cup.

What a joke it turned into. With those stupid things strapped on my legs, I wasn't as fleet of foot as usual. Every time I'd cross my legs over to turn, the damned guards kept clicking and clacking together. It was ridiculous. "To hell with this," I told Slats. "Just tie a harness to my back and tie the other end to the roof. Then whenever we get a power play and you need me in front of the net, you can just lower me from the rafters."

I got rid of the ankle guards. And Smitty didn't play lumberjack on my ankles. I'd known all along there really wasn't any danger of that happening because we'd come to a little arrangement after an earlier encounter.

Before we'd ever stepped onto the ice to play the Islanders for the first time, Bugsy Watson, who used to coach the Oilers before Slats took over, called me aside back in Edmonton and offered a little advice. "Watch out for Smitty," he said. I'd never heard about this Smitty guy, and I was really surprised when we got to Long Island and I skated out, looked around, and discovered that Smitty was a goalie. From what Bugsy had told me, I was expecting to encounter some great big guy who played wing or defence.

On my first venture deep into their end, I was skating around the Islanders' crease area when all of a sudden, whack, Smitty'd used the butt end of his goaltender's stick. I was off to the right of him, and he just lifted that thing up and cut me right underneath my eye. That did it. I didn't even bother taking my glove off. I just hit him and knocked his helmet, mask, and everything off. I don't know where they went — in the stands, for all I know. But there he was, without any protection. So I took my stick and was going to hit him with it but missed and broke the stick over the crossbar. Smitty got the message. For the rest of my career, he kept his stick away from me.

Goalies didn't like you standing there in front of their net, naturally. For one thing, you blocked their view of the puck, which put them at a distinct disadvantage. After all, if you're going to stop the puck, it does help to know when it's coming at your net. So they won't hesitate to use their stick to help persuade you to move. Some, like Smitty, would attempt to be real persuasive. Others went through the motions.

John Garrett was playing goal for the Quebec Nordiques one night when we were visiting the Colisée, and I was standing in front of the Quebec net. He kept tapping me on the back of my calves with his stick. From the players' bench, it must have looked like he was really whacking on me while he protected his crease. But those little love taps he was giving me wouldn't have broken a pane of glass.

"Sammy, don't get mad," John whispered through his mask. "The coach expects me to do this."

"Okay, no problem," I told John. I even moved out about six inches or so, just so Garrett's coach, Michel Bergeron, wouldn't get mad at him. But I made sure I didn't move far enough that Slats would get mad at me, either.

Slats wanted me in that goaltender's face, and I regarded that part of the ice right on top of the crease as my own personal backyard. A lot of players smaller than me would get cross-checked and banged out of the way when they tried to set up shop in front of the opposition net, but I never had that problem. Nobody really went out of his way to bother me. Defencemen wouldn't take a run at me and try to knock me out of there. Most would quietly move up beside me and lean toward me with a gentle push, almost as if they were pretending to try to move me. We'd push and shove a bit, but the hacking never got vicious. That was great by me. I figured that with both me and a defenceman out there on top of the crease, the goalie wouldn't see anything at all.

But the rules were simple enough. If they cross-checked me, that was a fight.

Jerome Dupont broke the rule one night. He was the only guy I can remember who ever did cross-check me real hard in front of the net. We'd gone into Chicago to play the Blackhawks, and I was trying to plug up the front when he caught me. I always made sure I had really good protection on my upper arms. Good job, too, because Dupont really laid one on me that night. I thought it must have been an accident. He was a rookie, and I figured he just didn't notice the number on the back of my sweater.

So I thought I'd let that one slide, as long as he didn't do it again. Two seconds later, he cross-checked me a second time. Enough was enough. I made up my mind to take him apart, right there, right then.

A hockey fight is not like a poker game. Everything about the fight is quick. In poker, you can sit back, watch the cards and put on your poker face to intimidate or bluff people. But on the ice, it's right now. In a second or two, at the most, you've bumped together, looked at each other, decided whether you wanted to fight, and then dropped your gloves and sticks and gotten into it. It's just boom, boom, then go sit down. A lot of times you might take a cheap shot from somebody and think, Oh, well, I'll get him next game or next week. But there's none of that hesitation when two guys are going to fight. It happens so quickly that you're into it before you realize it.

I almost felt sorry for Dupont that night because I might have caught him by surprise. He didn't have time to think about whether he wanted to get into it because I made the

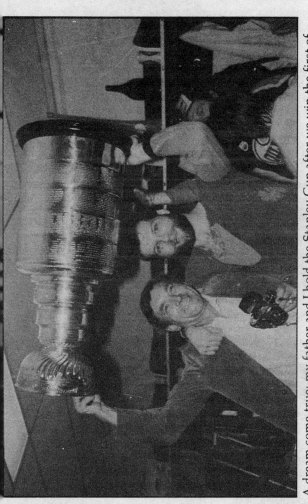

A dream come true: my father and I hold the Stanley Cup after we win the first of the Oilers' four championships, in 1984.

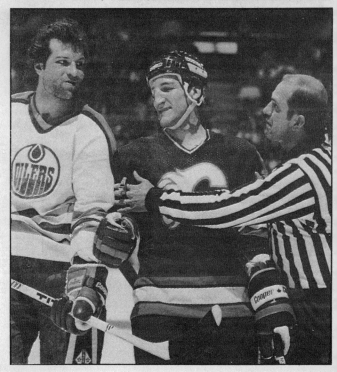

Close encounters with my nemesis, Calgary's Tim Hunter, in the Battle of Alberta.
(Top: Edmonton Sun; Bottom: Bob Mummery)

Gary Rissling of the Pittsburgh Penguins and I share a grin. (Edmonton Sun)

I went through all the right motions, but my heart just wasn't in it when I played my old team as a Hartford Whaler. (Edmonton Sun)

decision about fighting for him. I know all he was trying to do was play hard. His coach had probably told him to show some aggression in front of the net. That didn't mean I had to take it, though. I'd let Dupont get away with one cross-check and probably shouldn't have done that. Twice was out of the question.

It was an exhibition game, and as usual, the league was trying out more new rules. As a result of the incident with Dupont, I was tossed out of the game for being the instigator of the fight. Here's a guy trying to break his stick across my arm while he tries to move me. I get upset and put a couple of dents in him with my fist and I'm gone. Where's the justice in that?

But I could back off, too. You can read when a guy didn't want to fight. You can see it in his eyes. I'd like to think that I stopped a lot of fights just by looking at people. I'd glare at some guy, and if I got the impression he didn't really want to go, then I'd just keep glaring. Almost always, he'd back off, and we could get on with the hockey game.

Almost always. When he was with the Winnipeg Jets, Jimmy Mann and I bumped together, and somehow he lost one of his gloves. I turned around, looked in his eyes and could tell from his expression that he really didn't want to fight right then. But he realized he didn't have much choice.

We were in Mann's home arena. Everybody had watched these two tough guys bump together. And they had all seen Mann drop a glove, naturally assuming he was ready to start scrapping. Now they were waiting for some action. He couldn't very well bend down and pick up his glove. That would have been a little tough to explain to the home audience. It wasn't much of a fight. Mann was notorious for his habit of throwing this great big haymaker left, and when you know what's coming, it's not too difficult to avoid. What I remember most about the fight was how I could tell, before throwing a punch, that I already had him beat.

Most times, when there's a stoppage in the play and a couple of the heavyweight players from opposing teams wind up paired off, each with a couple of fists full of the other's jersey, they really have no intention of fighting. They're just dancing, keeping one another occupied so they can watch others square off. But you select your dance partners carefully. During a little scuffle on the ice in Minnesota one night, one of the smaller guys on our team grabbed Willie Plett of the North Stars and paired off with him, like everybody does when they want to stand around and watch a fight that's already going on between a couple of other guys. Willie is six foot going and 200 pounds, and he didn't appreciate some small guy embarrassing him by hanging on to his jersey.

"Don't grab me," Plett told my teammate. "If Semenko wants to grab me, that's okay. But don't you try it."

Willie just pushed my smaller teammate off to the side, skated over to me, and we grabbed hold of each other's sweater. We didn't do anything except go through the motions.

Nick Fotiu and I became good friends over the years, even though we were both supposed to be the big bad boys of our teams. He was playing for the Flames in Calgary one night when I was after Neil Sheehy, trying to get a piece of him. Nick grabbed me, skated me off to the side, and said, "Listen, he's not going to fight you, anyway, so don't waste your time. All you're gonna do is take a penalty."

"Yeah, I know," I told Nick. "But I'll try it. There's gotta be some way to get to this guy and cut the idiot strings on his gloves."

While all this was going on, there were thousands of people in the stands thinking that Nick and I were about to drop the gloves and go at one another. Never happened. We were pals.

But as much as friendship might have stopped a battle or two, more often the line was drawn by size. Nothing brought that one home more emphatically to me than watching Stan Jonathon of the Boston Bruins drop Pierre Bouchard of the Montreal Canadiens. We'd been eliminated from the WHA playoffs and I was in Florida, lounging around Soupy Campbell's bar in Fort Lauderdale. He had a big TV screen and a satellite dish, so we tuned in to the NHL playoffs. Bouchard was the Canadiens' enforcer, a real tough defenceman who was a huge local hero in Montreal. He stood a couple of inches over six feet tall and came in well in excess of 200 pounds. Jonathon was a fireplug. A short, squat guy at five foot eight who only weighed 175 but didn't have an ounce of quit in him. I remember that fight as if it had happened yesterday. Bouchard had him. He kept throwing punches, but he kept hitting Jonathon on the helmet. All of a sudden, Jonathon came up with two good punches that got Bouchard right on the beak and it was all over.

That did it. From then on, if I could find somebody six foot eight out there on the ice to fight, I'd go after him. Nothing's worse for the ego than to have some guy who stands five foot eight kick the shit out of you when you're six foot four. When Jonathon beat Bouchard, it didn't really accomplish a whole lot for Jonathon down the road. It certainly didn't secure his future. But Bouchard was the premier tough guy in the NHL at the time. He was as much a fixture with the Canadiens in Montreal as the CH on their sweater. But a "small" guy beat him and he wound up in Washington.

I was never kayoed. I was used to doing that to others. I'm thankful it never happened, because I have absolutely no idea what might have followed if they'd ever had to carry me off the ice on a stretcher after a fight. I don't know if I'd have said, "Put me back out there, Slats, and let's get this thing squared up right now." I'd like to think that I'd have been right back there. But who knows? I remember how embarrassed I'd been and how I'd reacted to being knocked down on the ice when I was a junior in Brandon. I never even got hit, and I was on the ice. But there was no way I was leaving that building without getting things settled. As it happened, I couldn't get at the guy I wanted on the ice, so I got him on the way to the dressing room. I couldn't contain myself then. But I was just a kid. How would I have reacted if I'd been twenty-nine or thirty and somebody smaller than me got a lucky shot in? I really don't know. Even tough guys mellow.

I was wary of Jonathon. I knew what he could do, and the same thing that happened to Bouchard could have happened to me. But I'd have fought him if push had ever come to shove. He certainly wasn't all that small. I certainly wouldn't have run away.

Occasionally you'd get drawn into a fight for a real strange reason. Like the time we were in Boston and I got tangled up with Terry O'Reilly, who later coached the Bruins. We were both on the ice when Jonathon squared off with my teammate Donny Jackson and was proceeding to give it to him pretty good. I knew Slats was going to be back on the bench pretty upset that Donny had lost a fight while I was just standing out there and not doing anything. And the fact that we were losing the game wasn't going to make Slats any happier. So I figured I had better get involved somehow. I kept reaching out, pushing Jonathon with the flat of my stick blade, trying to shove him off balance. I figured that would be enough to get O'Reilly to do something to me, then we could get into it. And it worked. The fight wasn't much. A little flurry of punches and it was all over. But it kept Slats off my case.

It's amazing how well people listen to one another down on the ice despite the noise of thousands of fans. I got as much mileage out of just looking at guys or talking to them as I ever did by fighting them. Probably more. That was just the way I liked it.

11

On the Road

To me, once the puck was dropped, playing hockey away from home was no different from playing at home. I could never understand "homers." What's the big deal about going into a different building? Why do people act tougher or more aggressive just because they're at home? Nobody's going to come out of the stands to help them. It shocks me to this day that some guys become real giants at home then turn timid on the road. I used to enjoy going to other rinks, where I could thrill to having people throw beer and programs at me. It made me feel right at home, especially during the early months of my pro career in Edmonton, when I wasn't exactly the most popular Oiler in the lineup.

It probably took a year or two before they stopped booing me in Edmonton and started to cheer. After a while, it got to the point that I would be given an ovation if I so much as carried the puck six feet. But it was intimidating to play in the Northlands Coliseum during those early days. Fifteen thousand people in one building can be a little scary when you're fresh out of junior and have never played before more than 4,000 or 4,500 people. We'd played a junior game in the Coliseum when I was with Brandon. The first thing I'd done when I got in there was run up to the top row of seats and look down at the ice. It seemed so far away — I couldn't understand why anybody would want to sit up there. How could they ever see the puck? But never did the thought cross my mind that someone would be sitting in that same seat someday, watching me play for Edmonton.

The first favor I'd ever asked Glen Sather for was to put me on the ice while my teammate Pat Price was out there. When I first went up there I was stumbling around a lot, and people didn't seem to like my style. I got booed a lot, but so did Pat. I figured if Slats would put us out there together, we wouldn't know who they were booing.

Later on, our home crowd made me comfortable. But it never made me feel any braver. I think that attitude goes back to junior days when I played for Dunc McCallum at Brandon. He never stopped stressing how important it was for us to play well on the road if we wanted to go on to the pros. What also helped was the travel schedule.

In the Western Canada Hockey League you travel from Brandon to Victoria on a bus. What's so tough about flying from Edmonton to Toronto when you've been used to thirty-hour bus trips?

In junior, they'd make you crawl out of bed before the birds got up, and you'd arrive at a rink at who knows what hour for the start of your trip. You'd handle all your own bags and everything, loading all the sticks and gear, too. If you didn't, it got left behind, and that would be a whole brand-new world of trouble nobody wanted to find out about. Then you'd get on the bus, unpack your clothes, hang up what you could, and try to close your eyes for a while and get as much sleep as you could.

On one road trip, our bus driver only lasted twenty miles. We were going from Brandon to Flin Flon, a ten- to twelve-hour trip, depending on the weather — which was almost always rotten — when the driver got real sick about twenty miles out of Brandon. Of course, there was no way we were going to turn around. One of the players, Murray Thompson, knew how to drive the thing, so he took over. The bussy climbed into Murray's sleeping bag and stayed there for days. He was sick all the way up there, sick all the time we stayed, and sick the whole way back.

After games, most times the bus was your hotel room. Chances were, you had another game coming up the next night in a town five or six hours away. That's the way it went, night after night, half the winter. You haven't seen lonely until you've seen a stretch of highway between Moose Jaw and Swift Current at four-thirty on a January morning.

In my last full year of junior with Brandon we went on an eight-game road trip and came home undefeated. In a seventy-two-game schedule, we only lost eight all year. But we ended up getting beaten out by New Westminster Bruins in the WCHL final. They had a big tough team and put an end to any thoughts we had of winning the Memorial Cup that year. We had a more talented team, but they'd get under my skin, and I'd get tossed out and then they could go about their business.

In the NHL you stay in the very best hotels and have your choice of many of North America's finest restaurants. Believe me, the road isn't anywhere near as tough as a lot of people would try to make you believe. But at the same time, after a few years, the glamour starts to wear off. You aren't going to New York to catch a play on Broadway. You're there to work. It can get to seem pretty tedious, and after a few years all the hotel rooms start to look the same and the plane rides start to seem a couple of hours longer than they used to.

A game is a game, whether at home or away. But some of the nights away could be pretty different.

One of my funniest memories is of me on my hands and knees in a hotel room in Saskatoon. When I played Tier II hockey with the Brandon Travellers, we never traveled. Well, we did, but we sure never stayed overnight. Five hours on a bus to Kenora, play a game, then back on the bus to ride home. Four hours to Dauphin, play, then four hours home again.

Where could we look forward to going with the Travellers? Nowhere, that's where. Because we never got a chance to hang around overnight to meet anybody or do anything.

Making matters worse, we just didn't have a good team. We had a lot of older guys around who really didn't care. They realized they weren't going to make it with the junior team and that their competitive hockey careers were all but done.

On our last road game, which meant nothing because we

were out of the playoffs, we had to go into Winnipeg to play St. James. I was sitting there minding my own business when some guys brought a bunch of wine onto the bus. For the ride home, I guessed. Little did I know. Turns out it was for on the way there. I don't know what ever possessed these guys, but they drank all the way to Winnipeg. By the time we went out for our warmup about six of them were hammered. Our coach, Elliott Chorley, hauled them off the ice, and by the time I came back into the dressing room, there were six guys standing under ice-cold showers. Elliott was trying to sober them up for the game.

A day or two later, the Wheat Kings called me up from the Travellers. I was to go with them to Saskatoon for the 1975 WCHL playoffs. This was big time, believe me. We went there for games on Friday and Sunday nights, and I thought one of the greatest things about the whole deal was that we'd be staying in the same place for three whole days. I could actually take my clothes out of my suitcase and put them in the drawers. It was like we were homesteading.

The coach said curfew was 11:00 p.m. and to me, it seemed like the Eleventh Commandment. Trouble is, I've never been much of an angel. I wasn't going to go out and see the bright lights. For one thing, I was seventeen and wouldn't have known where to find them. For another, it was Saskatoon. Besides, I was scared stiff of what they might do to me if I got caught.

But I was so excited there was no way in the world I could turn that light out at eleven and go to sleep, so I turned on the TV and turned the volume down; the only way I could hear the damned thing was to kneel right in front of the set with my eyes a foot from the screen. Every time I heard a noise from the hall I'd turn off the set, dive for the bed, and scramble under the covers. Two minutes later, I'd be back on the floor, watching this stupid Western movie. Years later, when I was wandering through the hotel lobby at about three or four in the morning, I'd think back to that night when I was so afraid of being caught breaking curfew and I'd start laughing. That's usually about the time Slats or one of the assistant coaches would appear out of nowhere to wish me a good morning.

But I had a lot of learning ahead of me at Brandon before I was ever going to have to worry about Slats. And it wasn't easy. Every night was a test. Every shift, sometimes.

If I'd had any say in it at the time, the WCHL games would have been on national television. The hockey seemed that good to me at the time. It was light-years ahead of anything I'd ever been involved with before. Later, after some time in pro hockey, I'd go back to Brandon and now and again I'd see the Wheat Kings play and think it all looked so disorganized. But things had changed. When I first started, teams weren't drafting a lot of underage players. Guys got to spend their whole terms in junior, so the caliber was a little higher than what it is today. Still, to go back and watch junior hockey after playing pro was to see the game from a totally different perspective.

Mind you, when I first went into junior, I was hardly in any position to say a great deal about organized drills and precision teamwork. I wasn't in position to say much about anything.

I was our tough guy. Everybody else's tough guy (or anyone else they had who thought he was tough) was going to test me. I had a hair-trigger temper at the time and was game to take them all on. Word about that sort of thing gets around from locker room to locker room fast. Players think twice about fighting you. A reputation isn't all bad at times, but you have to be ready to defend it.

The change from the juvenile who'd never had a fight to the tough-guy junior didn't happen overnight, but it didn't take forever, either.

Initially, the biggest battle I had was to get the weight on. At seventeen, I'd already hit the six-foot mark and didn't weigh any more than 180 pounds. I had to get some meat on these bones. I was getting all the exercise I ever needed. As if hockey wasn't enough, the club had arranged a summer job for me with a paving company. Try that on a July afternoon in southern Manitoba, and it'll give you a brand-new meaning to the word *sweat*. But I needed something else besides exercise if I was going to pack on some pounds. Food!

But getting it wasn't going to be easy. I don't remember the name of the family the Wheat Kings first boarded me with.

They probably did what they could to forget mine, too. These people were under the mistaken impression that they might be able to make some money by offering room and board to junior hockey players. And they must have, since lunch consisted of a peanut butter sandwich and supper was a potato, two or three forks of vegetable, and a little piece of something that looked like it might once have been a pork chop. There was another guy from the team sharing the room with me, and we both figured we'd better get the hell out of there before we starved to death. We were used to living at home, where our moms would be glad to make us as much of anything as we wanted. Nobody should count of boarding two teenage boys and making any money on the deal. But these people did, so my roommate and I decided to split in the middle of the night. What a couple of pathetic cat burglars we'd have made. With all the lights out, we were slamming doors, bumping into walls, and stumbling down the stairs with our arms filled with pillows and suitcases, giggling like a couple of silly schoolgirls. We got all our stuff into a car we'd borrowed and were all set to start it up and drive off, thinking we'd pulled the perfect getaway, when a voice from the house let us know we hadn't exactly been stealthy: "Hey, you two! Aren't you at least going to have the decency to leave the key?"

We went back and apologized. I hope they understood. Fortunately, Elliott Chorley did. And since he lived on an acreage where he kept some livestock and could use some help taking care of the place, he boarded the two of us. The fridge was always full. There were always steaks and ribs in the freezer. It was a teenager's paradise. The work wasn't easy. I probably never worked harder for my meals in my life, but it was good, honest work and did me a whole lot more good than harm.

Meanwhile, I was receiving my crash course in physical hockey. I don't ever remember anybody telling me to fight or play tough. It just happened. Somebody would usually come after me. I never had to be told to get involved. It was inevitable.

I changed quickly from the sixteen-year-old noncombatant. I had to. Poor Mom — she didn't know what was going on. She was really shocked the first game she came to see us play. There was a face-off and I told the guy from the other team who was beside me, "Look, I'm going to the net. Just get out of my way." He just stood there. So at the drop of the puck I elbowed him as hard as I could. Got him right in the ear and nearly took his head off, helmet and all. But somebody had been in the circle, so they had to repeat the face-off. Once again I told him to move. Once again he didn't. And once again I drilled him and be damned if there wasn't something wrong with that face-off, too. It happened three times in a row. He kept standing in there and I kept trying to take his head off. Mom was sitting in the stands in a state of shock, wondering what in the world ever happened to her son David. She'd just never seen me be that mean before.

Dad always understood that hockey's an aggressive game. He never considered me a goon. Nobody close to me ever did. They knew I had a little more talent.

There was a time, though, when I was thoroughly ashamed of myself, at the end of what was probably the most spectacular fight I ever got into during the years in Brandon. It was a real strange deal that involved Wes George, who played for the Saskatoon Blades. We'd squared off when he threw a punch at me. There were a bunch of fights going on at the time, and a couple of guys had fallen to the ice where they were wrestling right behind me. When I stepped back to avoid George's punch, I went tumbling back over these guys on the ice and fell flat on my ass with Wes right on top of me.

That was the ultimate embarrassment. This was the Keystone Centre. It was my rink. We owned this place. Here some guy from Saskatoon had wound up on top of me in front of my home crowd! And he hadn't even hit me with a punch!

I went nuts. Before we could even get up, the linesmen were all over us. One of them grabbed Wes, dragged him off me, and hauled him over to his team's gate. The other one tugged me over to our bench. We were both gone with game misconducts.

But I wasn't finished with this, not by a long shot. I'd have followed Wes all the damned way out to the parking lot if I had to. He wasn't getting out of town without me getting back for being embarrassed.

Keystone Centre was a bit of a unique building. George had to leave from one corner of the rink and I had to leave from another, but both our dressing rooms were located at the same end of the building and between the dressing room doors was an area that was almost like a big stage. So when I left the ice, instead of turning right toward our room, I turned left and walked toward Wes. It was like a gunfight. The showdown on Main Street, with both characters meeting head-on. We got into it right in front of the Zamboni on a concrete floor. People tell me they saw sparks from our skates flying all over the place as we wrestled around. It was a helluva mess.

I still get a shudder up my back thinking about the irreparable damage I might have caused. We'd had a real good scrap and we'd both thrown all the punches we needed to throw, but I didn't know when to quit. For a reason I still don't know — and for the first and last time — I jammed a finger in one of his eyes. It went in up to the second knuckle and I can remember thinking, Dave, what the hell are you doing? Get your hand out of there.

I'm only grateful I didn't cause Wes any lasting damage, especially since I had the chance to get to know him well when he spent a little time with the Oilers and we became good friends.

Once you got to pro, they knew what you were there for. They knew what you'd done in junior. I had a helluva lot more fights during the three years I played for Brandon than I did during the next three with Edmonton. In junior I had to go out and fight almost every night. The scouts were there and you wanted their recognition. As a pro, you didn't have to prove anything to the scouts. Only to a few other players.

12

A Little Help from My Friends

I was greener than the inside of Peter Pocklington's wallet when I first went away from home in Winnipeg in the summer of 1974 to play hockey 200 kilometers and one lifetime away in Brandon. I didn't have a clue what I was supposed to do next in this brand-new environment. For that matter, not much had changed by the fall of 1977 when I turned pro and went to Edmonton. Fortunately, wherever I went, I'd found a way to get all the "help" I needed. I'd hang around with the veterans.

I don't ever remember spending any great deal of time with anyone my own age. For some reason, I was always with the "older guys."

In junior hockey days, only a couple of those older guys might have reached the ripe old age of twenty-one. Most were only a year or two older than me, three tops. But they were veterans and I looked up to them. As for the guys who'd turned pro but would show up at our junior camp to work themselves into shape, they were almost gods. I couldn't get enough of hearing them tell stories about other pros and the big-league arenas and cities. I was in awe of those guys. One of the greatest pleasures I've ever had from hockey was to come back to Brandon from Edmonton after I'd turned pro in '77 and be accepted as "one of the guys" by many of those same pros. But that was a long, long way down the road for the kid from East St. Paul whose parents dropped him off in Brandon.

At that stage I was only seventeen and had certain rituals yet to learn about. Some things in western Manitoba are sacred. Partying during the May long weekend at Clear Lake, 100 kilometers north of Brandon, is high on the list. Most everybody seemed to go, including the hockey crowd. Especially the hockey crowd.

Sometimes a group of us from the junior team would just go up there and wander around the campground. We'd walk up and down the streets between the rows of portable cottages, tents, and house trailers. We'd hear noises from all the parties. Sooner or later, we'd stumble across a party that looked as though it needed our company. If we didn't, we'd go back to the tent we'd borrowed and create a party of our own.

Every now and again we'd luck out and meet some pro hockey players who'd come home to the area for the summer. They'd have their barbecue parties and when we ran into them, they'd always make us feel welcome. I was sitting in a trailer with a bunch of guys one night when Ron Chipperfield was there. At that stage of my life, I still didn't know what a Gretzky was. I only knew that hockey stars couldn't get much bigger than Ron.

Chip was a legend in Brandon, where he'd been the star of the Wheat Kings before turning pro with the Vancouver Blazers. I heard about him everywhere. He was a gifted centre, but there was far more to him than hockey. Ron had a winner's attitude, a certain class and air about him that set him apart.

So that night in the trailer at Clear Lake, I wanted to tell Chipper that I was going to make it someday, that somewhere, someplace, I'd play with him. Then I thought to myself, Naw, don't do that. You'll sound like an idiot. Imagine how many times he's heard some kid say that!

So I kept my mouth shut. But for a kid, rubbing shoulders with Dunc McCallum and Ron Chipperfield showed me how much fun success could be. From the first day I met them, I wanted my life to be like theirs. I wanted to pull myself out of the Brandon Wheat Kings' team jacket and into a suit.

Imagine my surprise, then, when I first turned pro and went to Edmonton. Who should come to my rescue and offer me a room at his place but Chip? Moving in with Ron, Joe Micheletti, and Brett Callighen took a big load off my mind.

Back then if you were called up from junior to an NHL team, there were certain rules the NHL Players' Association had negotiated that the clubs had to follow. Things like providing you with accommodation for a certain number of days. They had a different set of rules in the World Hockey Association: no rules. You were on your own.

But on that team, you were never lonely. In my case, Chip was there to help me find my way around without having to worry right away about getting a place of my own. Besides, getting to know those guys was hardly a problem. It was getting to understand them that took time.

Paul Shmyr might have been the worst-dressed hockey player of all time. No, that's wrong. He *was* the worst dressed, without doubt. And he was proud of it. Paul wore these tight pants with flared bottoms and short matador-type jackets. God knows why, but he liked that look so much that he had about twenty of those outfits made by somebody in Vancouver. They were all in different colors and he'd wear the most outrageous ties with them. He took a lot of heat from the guys about his wardrobe, but he reveled in it. He wore that stuff just to get a rise out of us.

I watched Paul play hockey on TV long before I ever went to Edmonton. I remember him playing in the Canada Cup one year. That television set can be deceiving, though. I was expecting this huge, tough, serious guy, and here Paul turned out to be a little guy, one of the funniest people I'd ever met.

I spent most of my time with the older guys: Al Hamilton, Jimmy Neilson, Ace Bailey, Bill Goldsworthy, Paul Shmyr. They took a liking to me and I got to know them quickly. They were all about ten years older than me, getting toward the end of their careers, while I was just starting mine. To be accepted by those guys meant quite a lot to me.

They were all tough and they could all fight. But why should they have to? There were younger guys around, like me for instance, who were there to do that stuff. These vets could play their own game without being called on to fight. To me, that's the way it should work. Those guys shouldn't have been expected to go out there and do all the fighting. They were established. They'd paid their dues. They just wanted to finish their careers. Besides, the rough stuff's what I was getting paid for.

They had all played in the big time. Bill Goldsworthy had been a fifty-goal scorer with Minnesota. Jimmy Neilson was a solid defenceman for years with the New York Rangers and had spent sixteen years in the NHL. Ace Bailey had been with the Boston Bruins and helped them win a Stanley Cup. I didn't know as much about veterans like Al Hamilton and Paul Shmyr, who'd played in the WHA.

But I soon found out that all of them liked to have a good time. They made the road a lot of fun.

Togetherness on the road is a big thing. Everybody would go for a beer. Even if you only stayed for one, it was a team thing. For years after practice at home, we'd always go upstairs in the Northlands Coliseum afterward to Champ's Restaurant and have lunch. It was our routine. Ninety-nine percent of the guys always showed up. It was nothing special. Just lunch, then go about your business, but I think it helped keep the team together.

These guys had more than their fair share of favorite watering holes on the road. On that very first trip, with me just three days out of Brandon and both my eyes filled with stars, it didn't take long for me to be baptized.

My first roommate on that first trip in 1977 was our goaltender, Smokey McLeod. If I live to be a million, I'll still be able to hear Slats when he climbed on the bus, handed McLeod the room list, and said, "Smokey, look after the kid. Keep your eye on him for me."

I was to find out in Birmingham a couple of days later that Smokey tended to take things rather literally. Chip, Butch Deadmarsh, and Smokey took me out to a place called Victoria Station where we had a huge prime rib dinner. Then we went to this club where, to be honest, I really didn't know what to expect. I was only twenty.

Chip had pointed this place out to me, right across the street from the Civic Centre Arena, when we'd arrived before the game. "There's where we're going after the game, Sammy," he'd said through a smile. I couldn't see why we'd bother. The bar looked like a real dive. When I first saw it, all I could think about was that I used to go into much nicer-looking places when I'd played junior hockey. Why, I wondered, would pros who make the big bucks bother with a joint like this? When I walked in I realized why. The place was filled with great-looking women, all dressed to kill. The only thing that surprised me more about the place is how anybody ever found the joint in the first place. Some hockey player had discovered it between the freeways one day and passed the word along. Next thing you knew, it was an institution.

I wasn't sure how long this good thing would last. My pro experience was still measured in hours at this time, and the eleven o'clock curfew Slats laid down seemed pretty ominous to me. I kept glancing at my watch, getting more and more nervous the closer it got to eleven. Finally, I walked over to Smokey and said, "I'm going now."

"No way, kid," he said. "You're not going anywhere. Slats told me to keep my eye on you and how in the hell can I do that if I'm here in the bar and you're back in the hotel. If I'm not going, you're not going, either. So just sit down and buy a round."

I was a rookie and pretty scared at the time. I sure wasn't going to get into an argument with a veteran like McLeod. So I had to wait until Smokey was distracted before I could sneak away. I didn't have to wait long, though. Smokey tended to get distracted real easy in places like that, something I was to learn pretty quickly myself.

I was hardly what you'd call innocent at the time, even though I hadn't exactly moved in these circles. Back in junior, right up toward the end of my final full year, I still wasn't convinced anyone was going to draft me. I hadn't bothered making any plans about what I might do if I wasn't selected. I was just going to play it out and see what happened.

During my last couple of seasons in Brandon, I'd known there was an odds-on chance some very prying eyes would be on me every night we'd play a hockey game. There was always a scout or two somewhere in the building, picking players apart with their pencils. The coach would know when they were at the arena, but he'd never tell us. If he had, all the coach would have had on the ice was a bunch of nervous individualists who'd destroy the whole team concept.

Dunc knew when I was being scouted. Bob Freeman came down from Edmonton in 1977 to check me out for the Oilers, on and off the ice. I didn't know until Dunc told me later that Bob had stayed in Brandon for a week, just watching me. Obviously, Bob must have gone to bed pretty early that week. If he'd known the whole truth about what was going on late at night, I doubt his report would have ever convinced the Oilers to draft me.

The major difference between the after-hockey hours in the pro leagues is the freedom. Nobody's going to baby-sit you. You get a set of rules, and if you screw up, you pay the price. We were big boys and we were expected to look out for ourselves. Which we did. Regularly.

Slats had a system where the fines would double and keep on doubling. If you missed curfew, it cost you fifty dollars. Get caught again, it was $100. I got up near the $1,000 level a few times. It reached the point where I quit trying to sneak back into the hotel. I might as well use the front lobby for coming and going because Slats was going to catch me, anyway.

Every time he'd catch me (and he caught me every time) he'd say, "I don't even know why you bother doing this, 'cause I know what you're gonna do before you do it." I was always determined to outsmart him next time. Never happened, though.

There's a bar in Vancouver named Sneaky Pete's. They're thinking about renaming it Not So Sneaky Sammy's. I'd never been in the place before, but three of us wound up there an hour or two after curfew when we were in town to play the Canucks. Stan Weir, Dave Hunter, and I all walked in together, but I grabbed my drink and decided to wander around and have a look at this place while they held down one end of the bar. Next thing you know, I'm standing in front of the elevator when the door opens and a whole bunch of

Japanese tourists come piling out. And even more of them were coming up the stairs. It seemed like there were a thousand of them. I couldn't move in any direction. They were everywhere! Don't ask me where they came from. Don't ask me what they wanted. But I'm six foot four and I was at least a foot taller than any one of these little guys.

So what happens? What do I see from my vantage point high above that maddening crowd? The elevator doors opening again. Great, I thought, more tourists. But who should take one step out of that elevator, then stop dead in his tracks when he looked me right in the eye? Slats.

He was too busy looking at me to even notice Stan and Dave. But they sure saw him and they made it out of there through the back door. Slats got pretty mad at me over that one, though. It wasn't so much catching me out late that bothered him. But he sure did get pissed off when I decided to stick around and finish my drink after he'd caught me. Another five minutes sure wasn't going to change the fine.

Slats was on us all the time not to embarrass him. We tried. But we put him in a bad situation one night in Montreal, when he caught a whole bunch of us after curfew in a popular nightspot on Crescent Street called the Sir Winston Churchill.

He was with a friend and suggested they stop at the pub. Sather's buddy said they should find another bar, that the Oilers might be in this one.

"No way, it's after curfew!" Slats said. "My boys won't be out."

They walked in and there we were, a whole bunch of us, including an assistant coach. Only the European players didn't get caught. They were hiding in the cloakroom.

I wouldn't have intentionally embarrassed Slats. Let's just say it's his fault for going to a bar where any curfew breakers would go. He'd played the game long enough to know where the players' hangouts were.

He was the kind of coach we learned to respect because he helped put a whole lot of money into our pockets over the years. But sometimes he could get to me more than any other human being ever did.

It started right off the bat, on that very first road trip in 1977. We went down from Edmonton to Houston with that great stop in Vegas. Then we went to Birmingham. It was a tough trip. There were a lot of fighters on every team in that old WHA, and I felt like I'd met most of them on that one trip. But the bonus came at the end. To cap this road trip, we were finishing it off with a game against the Jets in Winnipeg, where my whole family was going to be up in those stands to see me play professional hockey. Your basic big moment.

But there was a hitch. Right from my first practice with the Oilers in Edmonton my right knee had been aching. I'd been standing in front of the net when Dave Langevin came sliding in from the side, caught me, and twisted my knee. Two days later we'd left on the trip and I'd just had it wrapped, then gone out to play hockey.

We were in the dressing room about an hour before the game in Winnipeg that night when Slats came over to me. "Go out and test your knee in the pregame warmup and let me know how it feels," he said. "See if you can do it."

Well, there wasn't going to be much doubt, not in my hometown. I stayed out there a few extra moments to make sure I was warmed up and ready to go. Everybody else had gone back to the dressing rooms and I was just about to leave the ice when I heard the announcement on the public address system: "Not dressed tonight for the Edmonton Oilers, number 27, Dave Semenko."

Damned if Slats didn't have his mind made up all along. But that wasn't the end of it. For about nine years, he had something against me playing in Winnipeg. He thought I'd be nervous. I don't know if he did it to other guys in their hometowns, but every time we hit Winnipeg, he was leery about letting me play.

Even years later when we'd go to Winnipeg I used to have to go up to him before the games and say, "My parents aren't here tonight, Glen. They moved to Brandon. They don't live here anymore. I won't be nervous. Promise. You can let me play." For years, he wouldn't.

I was the youngest guy on the team during my rookie season with the Oilers. And at the end of the year, Slats told me, "Listen, I want you to check in with me every month. Call me up."

Well, I thought that was bullshit. I wasn't going to call

anybody and check in. So I never called Slats. Not once the entire summer. A couple of weeks before training camp, the Oilers sent out this little training package of things we'd be expected to do when we showed up for our fitness tests at camp. We had to do fifty sit-ups and fifty push-ups. And we had to be able to run two miles in under fourteen minutes.

Finally, one day my phone rang. Slats was calling me.

"Hello," I said.

"David, you sound out of shape," he replied.

I told him I was fine and when he asked me why I hadn't called, I told him that I thought he was just kidding. He said he wanted me to be sure I followed the program in the training package, because he was still a little concerned about my knee.

"The push-ups and sit-ups are no problem," I told him. "But I am having a little trouble with the jogging part."

"I was afraid of that," he said. "Is your knee acting up?"

"No, it's not that," I said. "It's the wind. My cigarette keeps going out."

He hung up on me. We went at each other like that for years. Slats won more than his share, that's for sure. But I won that round.

13

Let the Good Times Roll

There are a great many things you can do with money. Spending it was always my favorite. I was real good at that. Too good. And sometimes things tended to get a little out of hand. Especially when a guy like Curt Brackenbury was around. Of all the guys I ever hung around with, nobody ever loved fun more than Brack.

We had a team dinner in Edmonton one night at the end of a season. I took my wife to the party, then drove her on home afterward, and left again to go out with the boys. Brack and I closed every bar in town and we still weren't through. The party was just starting to roll. So we went down to the Westin Hotel, where my "financial adviser," Peter Spencer, was staying for a few days. We cleaned out the little fridge in his room. Then we made him change rooms so we could get at a new fridge and a fresh supply. Finally, in one of those moments of sheer idiocy, Brack says, "Hey, let's go somewhere."

I told him we could hop on an airbus and slide down to Calgary. That's less than an hour away. Or we could even go out to Vancouver.

But no, the season was history and Brack said he wanted to go to Tahiti.

We checked that out and just the airfare was going to set

us back about $2,000 apiece. So we came to the conclusion that maybe it wasn't really the best idea in the world. What we needed was a long, sensible look at the situation. After all, it had been a long, hard night of frolicking. We were going somewhere exotic. That much we'd settled. We just didn't know quite where yet.

What we needed was some semisober thought about the situation. So since it was still too early in the morning for the bars to open, we went into the Westin Hotel restaurant and convinced the people there it would be real nice if they'd mix us up a pitcher of frothy cocktails to help us think while we contemplated these nice warm places. I wanted to go to Florida but Brack didn't. He talked about South America, but I don't know a whole lot of people in Rio de Janiero and didn't care to go there. We couldn't make up our minds where to go. Finally, we decided to write down places on a list and number them from one to five. If we had any place on our list that matched the other's, then that's where we'd go. We came up with ten different places.

We were in one helluva lot of trouble with this when Billy Harris and the late Paul Rimstead of the *Toronto Sun* joined us. We explained our dilemma to them.

"What do you want? Warmth? Girls?" Rimmer asked.

"Yeah, that sounds good — we'll take both," we said.

So Harris and Rimmer put their heads together for a moment, then suggested that we go to Waikiki Beach in Hawaii.

"I know a travel agent, John Farlinger, who used to play with the Edmonton Eskimos," Rimmer said. "I'll give him a call and get your tickets arranged. All you're going to need is money."

Brack didn't have any cash on him and had no quick way of getting any at nine o'clock in the morning, but I had my financial man, Spencer, right upstairs in the hotel. So I phoned his room.

"I'm going to Hawaii," I said. "I need three grand right now."

"No, no, don't do that," Spencer said, going on to tell me how it would really set my budget off. That was a laugh. It's only too bad I didn't realize at the time that it was Spencer's budget that would have been set off. But he had little choice in the matter. We were right downstairs and he had to come up with a check.

Rimmer, who knew more people than anyone I ever met in my life, managed to get the check cashed at the bank next door where a buddy of his was the manager. So we were all set to go. But there was still one major obstacle. I couldn't figure out what in the world I'd tell my wife. I couldn't think of anything to use for an excuse. But Rimmer just laughed and said to tell her I was going fishing. He even said he'd cover for me, and he did. He wrote a column that appeared in the next day's *Edmonton Sun*, telling how he'd met Brack and me in a restaurant and how we were going to get away from it all after what had been a hectic hockey season by going up north to do a little fishing. I figured that would pretty well cover all the bases. The paper would be there the next morning to add to my story, so the coast would be clear. The two of us could take off.

Brack, of course, wasn't satisfied to let it all go at that. Whenever he gets something going, he likes to invite the whole world along to share in the adventure. Sure enough, we ran into Glenn Anderson, and when Brack told him we were headed for Hawaii, he wanted to come along, too. So while they took off to get their shaving kits, I went home and told the wife I was heading off on a fishing trip. I packed blue jeans, warm sweat shirts, cowboy boots, and all your basic stuff for roughing it in the woods. Not long after, Brack came knocking on the door, dressed in his cowboy garb and looking like a legitimate fisherman. We got into the car and hadn't gone a block before the sweaters and stuff disappeared. We hopped on the plane and flew to Honolulu. The first thing we had to do was go shopping. I couldn't pack anything that was too conspicuous, so I had to buy myself some sandals, white pants, and one of those colorful Hawaiian shirts. Perfect, now we were all set, ready to go on a tear. And we did. I was there for about five or six days. Brack and Andy stayed a little longer. I phoned home once but I was totally paranoid. I was telling my wife all about how rough it was up in northern Alberta, but I swore she could hear the ocean waves over the phone.

Brack couldn't resist the chance to pull a gag. He just had to be doing something to put somebody else on all the time. So that night after everybody else had gone to sleep, he went around the room and changed all the clocks. Next thing you know, he's chirping at Glenn.

"C'mon, Andy, wake up and hurry up," Brack shouts. "We've gotta get down to the beach. We're late and we'd better hustle if we're ever gonna get a good spot."

The two of them threw on their swimming trunks and rushed downstairs. They swam out to a floating dock and looked back toward the beach. It was almost empty. Finally, somebody else came swimming out to the dock and Glenn started complaining to the guy.

"Hey, this place is dead," Andy said. "Where is everybody? What did we ever come here for?"

The guy just looked at Glenn like he'd flown in from Mars and said, "Hey, pal, what do you expect at seven o'clock in the morning?"

Things like that Hawaii junket didn't happen very often, thank goodness, but whenever the opportunity came up to have a good time, I usually grabbed it with both hands. Even after being burned in my "money management" deal with Spencer, I didn't handle things anywhere near as well as I should have. Slats knew all about the troubles I'd been through with Spencer and he was very upset, to say the least. He told me that I should have known better, that the warning signs were all there and I should have acted on them. But all that was in the past and I had a future to worry about.

I'd been on a three-year contract at $110,000 a year and it had expired. This time I was going to work out my own deal with Slats, but I really wasn't concerned about negotiating. I was so far in debt at this stage, I needed a paycheck to get my head above water. Slats said he'd give me a $10,000 raise and that was just fine by me. I was just happy to get another contract, so I signed for another two years on that $10,000 raise, figuring that $120,000 was plenty. That's the contract I eventually took with me to Hartford in the option year. Then, in the final year of my career with Toronto, I made $130,000.

I spent it as fast as I got it. I went to Las Vegas a few times to clean up. And it worked. I got cleaned pretty good. When

Hartford finished first in our division in 1987, I got a pretty good bonus check. So after a quick stop at the bank, I was off to Vegas for three days with $5,000 in my pocket. By this time, my marriage had long since become history.

In the summer of 1985 I'd come home from the annual NHL players' softball tournament at Niagara Falls a day late, as usual. For some reason, Dave Lumley and I seemed to be the last ones to leave. It was the same thing every year. The circus had gone and left a few stragglers hanging around town.

My wife, Susan, had told me before I left Edmonton that she was taking the kids to visit her parents back in Brandon, so there was no urgency for me to go home. When we finally did get back, Lummer drove me over to my house from the airport. I opened the door, took one look inside and realized that I'd been robbed.

When I walked in and took a closer look, I realized it must have been a pretty picky robber because the only things left were mine. My VCR was on the television stand, right where her TV used to be. There was some rented furniture left. And my clothes. There was some mail, too, including a letter from a lawyer that clarified the situation.

I got curious a few days later and phoned Susan to find out what the terms of any reconciliation might be. She had three: stop going to the bars with the guys; clean up my act and come home at a respectable time at night; give up my girlfriend, Marvette.

I couldn't even make two out of three on that list.

So here I was in '87, checking out Las Vegas. I don't like any of the games they have there. But blackjack and craps really like me. Marvette would go to bed early and every now and again, I'd drop up to the room. She thought it was quite nice that I'd come up there to check on her occasionally. But really, I was there to dip into the drawer and pull out a few more traveler's checks. She caught on to that act pretty quick and from then on, whenever we went to Vegas, she used to hide money from me so we were at least guaranteed we could eat the last day.

I'd go to Las Vegas thinking I'd win but I'd never count on it. I'd just take what I thought I could afford (and I never did think too long or too hard about it). We'd have some incredible dinners.

Vegas was an end-of-the-season type of thing. If that city ever had an NHL franchise, it would be ridiculous. Half the league would be broke. It's amazing, but money meant even less to me there than it did anywhere else. To spend a few hundred dollars there just for dinner was nothing out of the ordinary. Besides, what was a couple of hundred bucks in Vegas? You could win or lose that much in two minutes. To go out for a $300 dinner in Edmonton was to do something really, really special. Matter of fact, it was pretty difficult to spend that much. But in Vegas, no problem. One meal at Gigi's in Bally's Hotel would take care of that item real fast. You could start by tipping the maître d' $20 or $30 on the way in. That would get you a seat in your own private little dining area where they'd close the curtains all around you. Then you'd have to have a picture taken for twenty bucks. After all, a person's got to have a souvenir. Then you'd have a cocktail or two before dinner, followed by a couple of $50 or $60 bottles of wine to accompany this incredible meal. Sip on the grape, dine, taste a little cognac afterward, then get your picture taken again for another twenty bucks, just in case your appearance had changed since you sat down to eat. Eventually, I'd come back to Edmonton with a baseball cap and cigarette lighter that had Las Vegas written on them as my souvenirs of the trip.

In New York you could breeze through a few hundred dollars in a night pretty easily. The first couple of years I refused to go out in New York. There was something about the city that I just didn't like. I didn't trust anybody there. I was paranoid about it. Besides going for a couple of beers at Charlie O's and a meal at one of the famous New York delis, I'd spend all my time in my hotel room or at the rink. After a couple of years, when I started going to clubs like Studio 54, Limelight, and the China Club with Gretz, Kevin, and Mess, I discovered how easy it was to spend money in the Big Apple, too.

Slats was pretty careful with us in New York, though. During the regular season, I can't remember many times

when he'd have things arranged where we would be in
Manhattan the night before a game. We usually were coming
from away out on Long Island and would get into the city
real late, after we'd played a game against the Islanders out
at Nassau County Coliseum. We'd just go straight to the hotel
and stay there before playing the Rangers at Madison Square
Garden the next night. But quite often that game against the
Rangers would be the last one on the road trip. Afterward
we'd get to go out until all hours.

I really used to like going to L.A. Just the weather alone
was such a nice break from all the other cities that were cold
and damp. You could just lie back and relax. You'd get a
restful feeling just going in there. I don't know about playing
there on a regular basis, though. After winning numerous
cups, I could see finishing off a career there. That would be
a nice way to ease into retirement. To throw on a pair of
shorts, then jump into your convertible and go shoot a round
of golf after practice in January would be a totally different
life, wouldn't it? The only time you ever get anything like
that anywhere else is when playoffs roll around and the
weather warms up. Down there, it's playoff weather all
season long.

And what a spot for clubs! My favorite's a place called The
Ginger Man, which is owned by Carroll O'Connor who
starred as Archie Bunker in "All in the Family." The bar-
tender there a is fellow named Merv Cohen, and whenever I
was visiting L.A. in the summer and had time to kill, I'd drop
by the bar and shoot the breeze with Merv. I was sitting there
one time when I recognized a voice behind me. It was Greg-
ory Sierra, who used to play Sergeant Chano on the Barney
Miller program. I must have been sitting there with my
mouth open, staring at him, when he looked at me and said,
"Hey, Dave Semenko, how ya doing? I'm really pleased to
meet ya." Don't think that didn't feel strange. Here I am, a
kid from East St. Paul, sitting in a bar in Beverly Hills when
some TV star recognizes me and says hello.

Everything about L.A. was different. Especially that Forum
Club in their arena. It's got to be the only bar in any rink in
the NHL that the visiting team always makes a point of going
to. A lot of rinks have different clubs in them, but the Forum

Club's special. It's right upstairs above the visitors' dressing room, and it was an automatic place to start out the postgame evening with a couple of libations while you planned your evening from there. The game was over and nobody ever made a big deal about who had won or what went on during the game. They totally disregarded all that. It was just a nice social club where you could meet afterward before heading to the Marina del Rey or wherever. That's laid-back California for you. No hassles. No rehashing the game. You'd walk up two flights of stairs from the dressing room and enter a totally different world. I can't picture any rink like that anywhere else in the world. They couldn't put enough games in L.A. on the schedule so far as I was concerned.

Funny, it seemed like every time we went to L.A. we'd always talk about going to see Disneyland. The Finns especially would want to make the trip all the way out to Anaheim from Inglewood, where we stayed by the airport. But that was such a long haul. Especially when the marina was right there in the vicinity, with all that water, all those yachts, and all those beautiful women. So it was always the same decision: let's head for the water — we'll catch Mickey next time around.

Pittsburgh's a place that might surprise a lot of people who think of it as Steeltown and nothing else. I loved it. It was really vibrant. There are a lot of nice little clubs and restaurants. It's totally different than what you might imagine. Boston I loved, too. I'm not really big on American history, but there's something special about that place you just had to enjoy. Philadelphia's another great city. We stayed out at the airport quite a bit and never got involved in downtown too much. We were stuck out there for years and never really realized what a great city we were missing until we stayed at the Hershey Hotel downtown during the playoffs against the Flyers one year. There are some great clubs and some pretty solid seafood spots down by the waterfront. Montreal . . . Vancouver . . . just remembering some of those places makes my tastebuds snap and my wallet ache.

One of the most pleasurable times in one of the most pleasurable places I've ever been didn't cost me much at all. It was a stop on the hockey trail, but it was a long way from the bright lights of the NHL cities. I'm talking about Wichita, Kansas, where the Oilers had a team in the Central Hockey League. What was I doing there? Fooling around, mostly. My one and only trip to the minor leagues during an eleven-year pro career was strictly a volunteer mission.

Most players wouldn't want anything to do with the minors. After all, if you've got a two-way contract, you aren't going to get paid anywhere near as much as you would in the big league. Your daily expense money is chopped almost in half. The hotels you stay in aren't anywhere near the caliber of the ones the NHL teams come to take for granted. The minors could be scary.

But ever since I had joined the Oilers, I'd always known I was going to make the big club when I went to camp. Edmonton couldn't send me down when I first signed because they had nowhere to send me. So I didn't have to go there and "make" the team. I just had to be sure I didn't screw up too badly.

When I came out of junior I thought I was ready and could move right into the pros without missing a step. Very quickly, I found out what a tough jump it is. It was frustrating, but I paid my dues. Sitting on the bench in the big leagues seemed a lot better to me than being in the minors, playing every night. I watched a lot of the poor guys who'd come up to the Oilers every once in a while and felt sorry for a lot of them. They'd pack up all this stuff and just begin to get themselves a taste of the good life that goes with playing in the NHL and visiting those fabulous cities. But they'd only get a few shifts. Before they had even had a chance to show what they could do, the writing was on the wall. Even if they had a good game, many times they were only called up to keep the minor league system happy. And sometimes if it wasn't for morale down below in the minors, the call-ups were to shake the big league team and prevent any complacency.

But I never had to worry about being sent down. I never had to sweat having my salary chopped drastically and missing out on all the action around the league. No matter what I read in the papers or whatever anybody said about how the Oilers might be looking for young blood, I knew I'd be there. I was in a unique situation: at the time, there wasn't anybody they had with the Oilers who could knock me out of that tough-guy role. Young players would come and go, but I knew I was going to stay. I didn't work any less in training camp and wasn't overconfident. I liked the good life but wasn't stupid enough to think they were just going to carry me along without me working and earning my keep. I always tried to do well in the drills. But I never had that feeling of fear in the back of my mind that I had to do something spectacular today or I might get cut.

Slats was always thinking about improving my hockey skills. He didn't have to worry about the other part. That took care of itself. My role was to be an enforcer. Still, sitting on the bench isn't fun. As the years went on, there were lots of times I just wanted to get up and leave. Especially after Slats had said to me, "Sammy, you're up next," then would change his mind because something happened to the flow of the game. I'd get home at night, pissed right off. Then I'd get up in the morning and it would be all forgotten and I'd go to practice.

I loved it. In practice I didn't have to worry about fighting anybody or anybody taking cheap shots at one of our players. I could just play hockey and try to be fancy if I wanted. I could just have fun. I'd let that practice help me get over the night before. I'd think, Today's another day, and forget all about quitting.

All the same, a guy's got to get his shifts. He's got to play. And early into the 1980-81 season, I was spending almost all my time on the bench. Ron Lowe had been injured and the Oilers were going to send him down to Wichita where he could play himself back into shape. Since I hadn't been getting much ice time, I said I wouldn't mind going with him because I was wasting my time in Edmonton. Slats was glad to oblige. If he'd only known . . .

We had a pail of fun in Wichita. Larry Gordon was the owner and I got along with him real well. Ace Bailey, a good friend, was the coach. So I thought I'd go down to Wichita, have a few laughs with my buddies, spend a few dollars in their restaurants, and play a little hockey. That I did, in exactly that order. Besides, I was getting a major-league salary in a minor-league town. Wichita was just one big party.

Some mornings I did wake up and wonder to myself, What the hell am I doing down here? What kind of a waste is this? Why am I not back in Edmonton where I belong? Then I'd go to practice and go out with the guys afterward. It was so relaxed. There was no pressure.

The fun day to end them all came when we showed up at the practice rink one afternoon and the ice was all screwed up. There was something seriously wrong with the ice plant. Huge chunks of the ice had broken up, so we couldn't work out. All the equipment bags were piled up outside the rink. Just then, our goaltender, Pete LoPresti, pulled up in his half-ton and came up with a great big cooler filled with ice-cold beer.

So there we were, sipping a cold beverage while we all lounged in the sun, lying on the equipment bags. No game to play. No practice to worry about. It was heaven. At that moment, a parking lot outside a hockey rink in Wichita was as good as any club in New York, L.A., or anywhere else on this planet.

"Hey, guys, I wonder how they're doing up in the Bigs?" we all laughed.

I was going to break in my new skates that day and there was still a fairly large piece of ice left in the middle of the rink. While the guys sprawled on the equipment bags outside suntanning, I put on my skates and took my stick, a bunch of pucks, a chair, cigarettes, and a beer out onto the ice. I sat there for quite a while, sipping and smoking and flipping pucks at the corner of the rink. It's the only time I've ever practiced in a chair. It was such a tough workout. I had to stop and go back out to rest with the other guys.

I think all athletes will say the same thing: no matter what city they're in, no matter what league their team belongs to and no matter what game they play, there's nothing better and no fringe benefit in sport bigger than having practice canceled. Nothing.

14

$100,000 — For Golf Clubs

When I'm asked how I did financially during my eleven years in professional hockey, the answer never varies: I broke even.

I only had a few bucks in my pocket when I first went to Edmonton in 1977 and my bankroll was pretty well the same when I left Toronto in 1988. It's certainly nothing to be proud about, but sadly, I wasn't the only one to end up in a leaky financial boat. Players today are setting up plans to further their educations because they have all this free time on their hands. Universities and colleges are cooperating because there's such a demand for these courses from prospective students. Everybody's getting into the act and the NHL is doing everything it can to help.

What a change that is from the way things were when I broke in. The only guy I know from those early days in Edmonton who had something when he got out of the game was Soupy Campbell. He had a deal to buy his bar in Florida all set up and brewing for a couple of years before he retired from the game. But even Soupy never made a big deal out of it. I can't recall one single teammate ever saying, "This is my last year and I'm gonna do this or that." Don't ask me why, but things like that never seemed to be brought up in the conversation. Nobody seemed worried about tomorrow. Everybody was living for today.

When I was about to leave Brandon and turn pro, Ron Simon of Minneapolis handled my contract negotiations with the Minnesota North Stars and Edmonton Oilers. Ron had done some work for other pros who had come out of the Wheat Kings' organization and he set up a two-year deal for me. He also advised me to get some of my money put into annuities, so I'd done that. And things were rolling along quite nicely until the day I met Peter Spencer, who was to become what I will laughingly call my "financial adviser."

You've heard the expression: "Take the money and run." Well, Spencer did. All the time he was in charge of my finances, I never did know what he was charging me. I found out later it was 100 percent.

I met Spencer through a teammate in Edmonton, Pat Price. We were sitting around the dressing room shooting the breeze after practice one day in September 1979, when Pat asked me if I had anybody taking care of my business interests. I didn't, so when Pat said he had a meeting set up at the Château Lacombe that night with a friend of his from the West Coast who was into money management, I figured I might as well go along and see what was happening. I wasn't the only one who was interested. Two other teammates, Ron Lowe and Doug Hicks, came along, too.

We met with Spencer and he told us his goal was to get a few of us hockey players together, then pool our resources and make some various investments. Whatever he was talking about was over my head. He was going to flip this and flop that and we were all going to come away wealthy. And that was just fine by us.

I never did like the guy's personality. I don't know what it was. Nothing specific that I can recall. But there just seemed to be something about the man that was annoying. Still, I thought, What do I know? Maybe this is the type of personality that all the money-makers have. So I let it slide, figuring it was all part of the scene, and tried to have as little to do with him as possible. I even went out of my way to avoid meetings with Spencer when he'd come to town. Ron Lowe acted as a go-between. He'd meet with Spencer, then bring whatever message Spencer had back to me. I wasn't worried.

The money was always there when I wanted some and that was my only concern.

I signed some sort of document so my money from the Oilers went directly to his Spencer Management Company with no taxes taken off. All the tax was going to be paid, supposedly, at the end of the year. So all this tax-free cash went directly to Spencer. It seemed we were always talking about being on some sort of budget but it never happened. I never, ever had any documentation of where my money was and what it was doing, and stupidly, I went along on some sort of blind faith. I just didn't want to be bothered. I had it in my mind that I was just going to play hockey. I didn't want to worry about money. Just take the paychecks, give me what money I need to live on, and make me more with the rest.

Granted, there were times when it appeared a little desperate. But Spencer always managed to get the money there somehow.

This went on for two years.

When I first signed with the Oilers, I'd agreed to a two-year contract that went from $45,000 for my rookie year up to $48,500 for the second season. During the next three years, I'd worked my way up to about $85,000. But in 1982, I'd become a free agent with compensation and Spencer said he'd handle my negotiations. No thanks, I told him. I'll go this one on my own. Why was I going to do that? Simple. Because Slats had told me to come on in and talk with him, friend to friend, and never mind about bringing any agent along. Good old Slats. What a great guy he was.

So I went into Sather's office and tossed out a figure. Nicky Fotiu of the New York Rangers had come through town that summer to play in an exhibition ball tournament and he and I spent some time together. One of our conversations got around to salaries, and Nicky let me know he was making somewhere in the neighborhood of $150,000 in American money to play for New York. Well, I told Slats that since I was filling the same role in Edmonton that Nick filled with the Rangers, I should be making as much money as Fotiu.

"That's bullshit!" Slats said. "I'll kiss your ass at center ice if Fotiu's making any 150 grand!"

Well, I thought, there goes that leverage; he's called that bluff. But it was no bluff. That's really what Nick was making, and Slats probably had a pretty good idea it was all along. But he wasn't going to give me any $65,000 raise to bring my salary in line with Nick's. Benevolent soul that he is, though, Slats did offer me a $1,500 raise. That was it, he said, fifteen hundred bucks and he was going to stand by it.

Well, right away I figured I'd better get somebody else in there to handle this business for me because it was all too apparent that I didn't know the first thing about negotiations. Besides, I was intimidated enough just sitting across the desk from Slats. That always made me feel nervous. I was totally out of my element in there. He's a master negotiator and to this day I feel uneasy in his office. Slats likes to let you know he's running the show. We'd known each other for a decade and joked around at times, but over the years we never really sat down and shot the breeze.

Our relationship was strictly hockey. And you couldn't be too candid, since what you said might come back at you at a later date. Perhaps in a few years, when I'm more comfortable out here in the real world, I'll be able to talk to Sather without feeling uncomfortable. I've seen Slats in every different phase: coach, GM, boss. He always seems to be thinking about something, and for the life of me, I could never figure out what it was. He was helpful to me, so far as worrying about what I'd do after my career. Whenever I'd get in trouble, and I was constantly screwing up, he kept sticking with me. He used to tell me, "I treat you better than I treat my kids." He was always trying to keep me on the straight and narrow. He'd do all these things for me and I'd end up dumping on him again somewhere down the road. I always felt bad about it. I never did it intentionally to hurt him. It just always happened, always at the most improper time.

Sather had played the game very differently than I did, both on and off the ice. He was very businesslike. When I think back to his career, he'd been traded all over the place and had run around causing all sorts of shit on the ice. But all the time he was planning for the future. He was a businessman, even back then. That was his approach. He was always worried, every day, about being sent down to the minors. He used to tell us that if he had a bad practice he was afraid of being sent down. Me, I didn't have a care in the world. I didn't worry about roles. I didn't worry about money. I didn't worry about anything. Slats couldn't understand that way of thinking. It was totally foreign to him.

Since it was obvious Slats wasn't going to give me much, I figured I might as well get Spencer to go in there and have a shot at it for me. Next thing you know, the papers were full of reports about how I was going to go to the Los Angeles Kings.

Spencer said he knew George Maguire, the president of the L.A. Kings, would offer me big money. I didn't know anything about what was going on. I was operating strictly on Spencer's word. Every once in a while, starting late in the season and going on all the way through the summer, he'd tell me negotiations were going on. He'd say Sather had upped his offer substantially, and Spencer threw around figures like $200,000 U.S.

I was in L.A. that summer going out with a girl from down there when I ran into Dr. Jerry Buss, then the Kings' owner, at a nightclub. One of the people in his entourage came over to me and said they'd love to have me come down to L.A., and they'd be willing to pay whatever I wanted. Normally, I'd have passed it all off as nothing but bar talk. But these negotiations were going on, and I had this $200,000 figure in my head. Edmonton hadn't won anything yet, and they sure weren't going to pay me that kind of money. If L.A. had offered me that $200,000, I probably would have jumped at it and gone south. Let's face it, that's a lot of money. But then I would have looked back to Edmonton, seen those guys winning those Stanley Cups and that would have bothered me to my grave. To miss that opportunity just for some quick money would have been disastrous. If I'd gone to California and gotten into that lifestyle down there, I'd probably have been finished in two years. Fortunately in Edmonton I had a coach and GM whom I lived in constant fear of. I was always afraid of screwing up and getting disciplined. I pushed it, sure, but never too far. Down in L.A. I could easily have gotten lost in the shuffle and never been heard from again.

Those contract negotiations seemed to go on forever until Spencer had me meet him at the Edmonton Inn one day to explain where we were. But I still wasn't satisfied. I wanted another $5,000. During all this time, I wasn't answering my phone. The reporters were constantly calling, but I didn't want to talk about the negotiations with them. As training camp drew closer, I made up my mind to hold out.

The morning training camp was due to open, Sather was trying to phone me at home. He was going to offer me the $5,000 I wanted, just so I'd be out on the ice with everybody else when camp opened. That way it would save him a lot of aggravation because he wouldn't have to get bombarded with questions from the press. Trouble was, I still wasn't answering the phone. I honestly didn't think Slats would call. If I had answered the phone that day and he'd said that I should just get down there, get on the ice in time, and I'd get the extra five grand, I'd have been right there. As it turned out, I ended up holding out for two more days and never did get that extra $5,000. It probably didn't matter because though I didn't realize it at the time, Spencer likely would have blown the five grand for me, anyway.

The tip-off finally came from NHL security. Slats called us all to a meeting in his office. He told us that something had been going on, that Spencer had been screwing around with different banks.

That was the last thing we wanted to hear. We told Glen that he must be mistaken. That's the crazy attitude I took, probably because I was so frightened that it might all be true. I figured if I ignored the bad news, it would go away. But, of course, it all came crashing down around us. And it came from every direction.

The wheels fell off. Literally! I'd been driving a '77 Trans Am and wanted some new transportation. Spencer said he could swing a great deal for me on a brand-new Bronco. He said he got a good trade-in price on the Trans Am and I'd only have to pay $4,000 difference to get the Bronco. I assumed he'd just take the difference out of my money that he had sitting there. Meanwhile, he kept the car, took out a loan for $15,000 in my name on the truck, made a couple of payments on it, then left it at that. So there I was, out my Trans Am with the bank chasing me for my truck. I actually hid the Bronco in Ron Chipperfield's garage for a while. But that wasn't doing any good, and I eventually told them where they could pick the damned thing up. I finally did get my Trans Am back, though. They shipped it back to me from Vancouver. I had to pay the shipping costs, of course. And I had to pay some strange costs out in Vancouver. It seems Spencer had my Trans Am stashed out there. Maybe he figured he might need a fast getaway car or something.

Crazy how it all works out, isn't it? I go through all that to get myself a new car that I can't keep. Then, years later, Gretz goes to the 1989 NHL All-Star game, wins a brand-new Dodge for being the star of the show, and gives the car to me. Gives it to me! Who says there's no justice in this world?

I've talked to Danny Gare and Ron Lowe about the financial mess we found ourselves in. Nobody really knows if Spencer set out deliberately to scam us or if he'd possibly been trying to make some good money for us when some investments went sour and caused him to panic. We just found out he'd been shuffling money between bank accounts all over the country, covering a debt here with money from somewhere else. He even had us sign for an American Express Gold Card and a prime-line credit account with the Bank of B.C. Spencer convinced us that he'd put his company on the line and that without his "in" at the bank, we'd never get this $25,000 prime American Express Gold Card. We probably could have done it on our own wearing Hallowe'en masks, but he had us convinced we'd never get the cards without him. So Ron Lowe, Doug Hicks, and I signed for these cards, without ever realizing that Spencer actually had the power to borrow against them. Two days later, he pulled out $75,000 from our three cards to pay off some other debt he'd rolled up somewhere else.

I had a $30,000 annuity that was paying me more than $300 a month. Spencer went to the bank and said, "Okay, how much money can I borrow with these $300 payments coming in?" They gave him $18,000. Thing was, there was a hitch — something about my middle initial being screwed up on the form, and the bank held on to the money coming in from the

$300 interest payments. The money wasn't going to pay off that $18,000 loan, but it wasn't coming to me, either. It just sat there accumulating all sorts of interest, all the way through Spencer's trial on fraud, theft, and uttering false document charges. I remember thinking that at least I was going to have this one annuity left. Turns out I had to let that go, too, to knock down my payments on all the back taxes I owed to the government because Spencer hadn't sent them a dime on my behalf.

He was a real beauty. One time in Vancouver I went up to his office. This was unusual, because I'm still not sure he ever had one. I think it belonged to a friend who was out for lunch at the time. Spencer said he had an office in Calgary, too, where he had this leasing company. A fellow from the RCMP commercial crime unit checked that one out and it turned out to be just a vacant lot. Strange, but if any vehicle of mine ever needed fixing or a few days in the garage for something or other, Spencer would always arrange another vehicle for me through his leasing company. Somehow I always got them off that vacant lot.

How much total? I'd say it cost me, over the course of it all, $100,000 cash. So a guy's got to make about $200,000 to clear that much. It was a real pain in the ass, not to mention in the wallet. First you make the money, then you have to make more to pay it all back. Then you still have to make some more so you have something to live on. Hey, I'm not saying I wouldn't have blown it all, anyway, but I thought I had a nice little retirement fund going.

They got me for more than $40,000 in back taxes, plus $11,000 in penalties and interests. They docked $1,000 a month off my paychecks for a long time. I was still paying right up into the summer after we won our second Stanley Cup. We'd made some arrangements that the government would be paid directly out of the money I had coming from the Oilers. I can't tell you how nice it was when I got the statement of all my bonuses for the 1984-85 seasons and there was still some money left for me. I'd finally paid it all off.

None of us who'd been tied up with Spencer for just over two years realized how deep the financial hole was. To this day, I don't know where the money went. I just know it didn't come to me. It took me two years of salary and a couple of Stanley Cup championships to get the Spencer financial monkey off my back. In 1984, when we won our first Stanley Cup in Edmonton, I made $36,000 gross in bonuses: $25,000 from the league and $11,000 in team bonuses from the Oilers. I never saw a cent of it. Not one damned penny. The government took half at the time, and later on they took the rest to pay off my back taxes. After we'd won the second Stanley Cup the next year, I finally managed to clear off my back taxes totally, and after everything I was left with $8,000. Eight grand might not seem like a helluva lot to show for two Stanley Cup championships, but I was happy about it. At least I got to keep something the second time around.

It was one hell of an adventure while it lasted. Real fast-lane stuff. I'm never going to forget the time Ron Lowe and I flew out to Christina Lake in B.C. where Spencer had a cabin. Pat Price, Ron, and I decided we'd play a little golf one day at the local course where Spencer was a member. When we got to the clubhouse, I mentioned to Pat that I'd have to rent some clubs.

"No way," Pat said.

Then he led me over to the displays and we picked out the most expensive set of irons they had in the pro shop. And the most expensive set of woods. And the most expensive bag.

"Put it all on Spencer's bill," Price told the golf pro. I laughed then, never realizing how much I was going to end up paying for the gear. The bill was ridiculous, but I've still got the equipment. Those golf clubs are the only material thing I have to show for my relationship with Peter Spencer. I like to tell people I've got a $100,000 set of golf clubs.

And the damned things still don't work!

15

Fight or Flight

Don't cry, I kept telling myself. Whatever you do, don't cry.

The plane was getting closer to the Edmonton International Airport and Sather's words kept pounding in my ears. "I've traded you to Hartford . . . call Emile Francis . . . here's his number . . . I've traded you to Hartford."

It was the biggest shock of my life. When I got off the plane, I tried to be in good spirits. I was humming that dumb Hartford Whalers' theme song. The reporters who traveled with us recognized the tune right away and they were having a good laugh. I was faking it and doing all right until Bob Freeman came up to shake my hand.

"We'll still be friends, right?" Bob said.

And that's when I lost it. Bob had been the first guy to meet me when I'd come to Edmonton from Brandon as a twenty-year-old kid, fresh off the junior hockey league bus. Now here he was, a couple of months more than nine years later, saying goodbye. There was no more holding back the tears. My eyes got all wet and I headed for the door. No live interviews, thanks. The last thing I wanted to do was start bawling in front of the cameras. So I did all my farewell interviews over the phone, just in case.

I'd always told the guys that when I retired, I wanted them to Plexiglas off my locker room stall with a little wax figure of myself in there. I'd always called that stall the Shrine. Sure enough, the Oilers' assistant trainer, Lyle Kulchisky, set everything up. He'd searched around the back rooms of the Coliseum and had come up with a sheet of Plexiglas to put in front of the Shrine. And he'd filled the stall with all sorts of stuff: pictures of me and statistics from all my years in Edmonton. Lyle had even put a toy bus in there — a reminder of that incident in Boston when Slats had climbed all over my case for some reason nobody could ever figure out. I guess the guys had a good laugh when they saw Lyle's handiwork, but it didn't stay there long. Slats got a look at it all and told Lyle to get rid of it.

Meanwhile, I was off to Hartford. And the welcome was a whole lot different this time. When Bob had first met me in Edmonton, he'd driven out to pick me up at the airport, talked to me all about the city, and offered to help however he could if there was anything I needed. There wasn't anyone at the airport in Hartford when I got in during the dead of night. Just me, some sticks, and the clothes I'd packed for what turned out to be a four-month road trip. Since I didn't know what else to do, I went up to my room and turned on the TV. Finally, Emile Francis called and told me he'd meet me in the morning for a cup of coffee. It was the longest, loneliest night of my life.

Dave Lumley had gone to school with Don Cox, who was managing that hotel in Hartford, and had phoned ahead to say a buddy was coming down. Don took real good care of me. He gave me two adjoining rooms, which was real nice. The next day I met my new teammates, got my gear, and had a chance to work out with the team. Everything seemed to be going along just fine until I stood up at the bench during the national anthem before my first game as a Whaler. I looked down at my uniform and there was this big W on the front of my sweater. And it all hit me. I can't do this, I thought. I can't play for another team. I'd worn the Oilers uniform for so many years, I felt like ripping this one off and going back to Edmonton right then. I didn't care if I ever played hockey again.

But real early in the game John Anderson was hurt. He'd been playing on Hartford's first line with Kevin Dineen and

Ron Francis. So they put me out there to take Anderson's spot, and I scored a goal in the second period. The crowd really got behind me and that helped a lot. I needed them, because I hadn't been on skates for almost a week. I'd only had one practice with Hartford and that hadn't been much. It was nothing compared with the workouts I'd been used to in Edmonton. One of the Whalers told me in the locker room that if I sweated during practice in Hartford, it would be strictly my own fault. Jack Evans ran his practices almost exactly the same way every day, and they didn't amount to much more than public skating. It didn't take long to catch on to the routine.

But by the end of that first game, I was dead. I felt like I'd never skated so much in my life. It was a great start, though. I ended up scoring twice in that game, was named first star, and thought it was all too good to be true. Afterward, I told one of the reporters I thought it was amazing how many major changes in your life you had to go through just to get a couple of goals in this league.

Hartford plays in the Adams Division with the Montreal Canadiens, Boston Bruins, Quebec Nordiques, and Buffalo Sabres. It was my type of division, the perfect brand of hockey for me: tight-checking and really defensive. It wasn't anything like the freewheeling Oilers and the rest of the Smythe Division. We went into Boston and won. Then we went to New York and won there, too. It didn't take long for the inevitable to happen. I soon slipped right back into my "so you think you're a hockey player, do you?" syndrome. I got away from the style of hockey that had kept me in the league all these years, tried to get fancy, and never was all that effective there again.

In March we went to Edmonton, my first trip back to the Coliseum since the trade, the first time I'd seen all my friends since I'd left them at the airport in December. And some of the things I heard when I returned to Edmonton came as a shock. People actually expected me to go out there, grab Wayne, and beat up on him. I heard that sort of talk before the game from a number of people. At first I was totally convinced they were joking. Bad joke, too. Then it dawned on me they were serious. For the life of me, I can't understand what would possess someone to think something like that. If anything, why wouldn't they think I'd go after Sather? He was the one who traded me, not the players. But to think that I'd go out on the ice and try to get back at the Edmonton Oilers by beating on Gretz! What was that going to prove? That they missed me? That they really need me in Edmonton because Wayne wasn't protected anymore? It was ridiculous. It was quite a night, though. The people made me feel so welcome. The Oilers won it 4-1, and it was almost as tough to leave with the Whalers after the game as it had been to go to Hartford in the first place.

The Whalers won the Adams Division that year, finishing one point ahead of the Canadiens, and people were making noises about the Whalers eventually meeting the Oilers in the Stanley Cup final series. I didn't believe it myself. It just didn't seem possible. Besides that, I couldn't get excited about perhaps winning a cup in Hartford by beating Edmonton because, deep down, I still considered myself an Oiler. I certainly didn't have any long-standing loyalty to the Whalers. In fact, I didn't even know if I was going to be back with them the next season and kept getting feelings I wasn't in their plans.

Eventually, after Quebec eliminated Hartford in the division semifinals, Francis said they might offer me a termination contract, where I'd play another season then become a free agent at the end of the year. I figured I'd have to come back to Hartford and fight like mad for a job, just to get protected. And if they didn't protect me, then somebody would pick me up in the waiver draft. I tried to negotiate a two-year, one-way contract with Francis, but he said the Whalers weren't going to go for that and the best they could offer me was one year, with an option, on a two-way contract. Did I want to go there and beat my head against a wall trying to win a job? Did I want to take the chance of ending up in the minors? Did I want to go to Hartford's training camp, only to be left unprotected and end up hopping on an airplane to go to another city and another camp? No thanks. I figured if I just stayed home in Edmonton during the late summer of 1987, somebody would grab me and offer me a deal. I was willing to take my chances.

Shortly before training camps were due to open, the Toronto Maple Leafs came into the picture. That summer my old pal Curt Brackenbury had been visiting Edmonton and we went out for dinner. Brack said he was going through Toronto and would be seeing his old teammate John Brophy, who was coaching the Maple Leafs. Brack wanted to know if he should put a good word in for me.

"Don't say anything about having talked to me," I told Curt. "I don't want to sound like I'm begging for a job. But sure, find out if there's any interest."

I never did hear from Brack about what he might have talked about with Brophy. But not long afterward, I heard that Toronto had swung a four-player deal with Chicago Blackhawks that brought Al Secord to the Leafs. I figured I might as well forget all about Toronto since now they had their tough left winger. But surprise, surprise, the Leafs still wanted me. I was sitting at home in Edmonton, skating a little and working out a bit but nothing overly strenuous. I thought I had lots of time left to get myself into playing shape because I didn't intend to go to Hartford's camp. All of a sudden the phone rang and it was my good friend and former Oilers teammate Garry Lariviere, who was an assistant coach with the Maple Leafs. He told me Toronto had made a trade with Hartford, sending defenceman Bill Root to the Whalers in exchange for me. My initial thought was "Now I've got to get in shape in a real hurry." So I told Garry I hoped nobody was expecting any miracles and that I'd need some time to work on my conditioning when I got down there. The more I thought about it, the more it sounded like a perfect situation for me. To start with, John Brophy liked rough, aggressive hockey. This is going to be a dream, I thought.

How I wish I'd known what a nightmare lay ahead.

The way Brophy treated Chris McRae was the first tip-off. You can't meet a better guy than Chris. He's got a great heart, and all he ever wanted to do was make a decent living playing hockey. He isn't big but he's game. All Brophy wanted him to do was throw the muscle around. Nothing else. One night we were playing against the Red Wings when Chris came skating back to the bench and Brophy started going after him because he'd tried to go after a loose puck.

"Don't even look at that f----- thing when you're out there!" Brophy yelled at McRae. "Don't even think about the puck. You're out there to stir something up. Go fight Joey Kocur."

Can you believe that, from a coach in the NHL? Here's a guy who went out, worked hard, went up and down his wing covering his man and covered his point. But the puck sprang loose once, he made a move for it, and he gets it from this guy behind the bench. The game's supposed to be fun. You're supposed to be involved. Sure, with the role I had there wasn't a lot of "fun" at times, but deep down you want to be a player. You want to do something to help the team win. And even though what I was doing helped our team, I wanted to do it on the other side of the fence; I wanted to make the big play or score the big goal. Everybody does. That's hockey. It's what we were raised with all our lives.

Then you get to the Toronto Maple Leafs in the NHL and here's some kid getting a dressing down for trying to do something with the puck. It starts to eat away at you. I couldn't say to Chris, Hey listen, screw Brophy. Just go out there and play your game. I knew that if Chris didn't do what Brophy told him to, they'd send him back down to the minors. They weren't going to send me down. They weren't going to send somebody down when they figured that guy could cause havoc every time they threw him out there. And that's exactly the way the Leafs felt about me. Brophy expected me to be this atomic bomb, sitting on his bench, ready to explode when he pushed the button.

During the 1987 exhibition season in a game against Detroit, Garry Lariviere had told me before the game about some kid who was up from the minors who might just jump me. Sure enough, on my first shift the puck came around the boards to me from a face-off on the other side of the ice, and just as I started to turn to pick up the puck, the kid was there, all ready. He threw one and caught me. It didn't faze me all that much, and we got into a bit of a fight. I didn't realize until I was in the penalty box that I was cut above my eye.

That did it. There was something to be settled here. So after I'd been stitched up, I kept looking for the kid until I found him. I had him on the boards, pinned just where I wanted, when all of a sudden our players' box door opened up and we went tumbling through the opening, with the kid landing on top of me. Even that was no big deal. When we got to the dressing room between periods, Brophy stood in the middle of the room, waited until everything was quiet, then looked at me and said, "Semenko, I didn't get you in here to lose fights. What the hell do you think you're doing?"

Nobody had ever said anything like that to me before. It even took my teammates off guard. I told Brophy he'd damned well better put me back on the ice again then, and when he did, I squared off with the kid and opened him up pretty good. But the kid was only a target. It was Brophy I was mad at. He's the one I would have liked to fight. I couldn't believe he'd say anything like that to me and should have known right then that that's exactly what he was like.

Things just went from bad to worse. Eventually, it got to the point that I knew I wasn't going to play. Brophy only wanted me there for one reason: to fight. I'd never been sent out on the ice to fight before in my life. Anything that had ever happened had been spontaneous on my part. No more, though. One night Basil McRae elbowed our centre, Ed Olczyk, and to Brophy it was a simple matter of "Let's get Eddie off there and, Dave, you go out and take care of McRae." I didn't need that. I didn't feel comfortable. I wasn't really mad and unless I'm mad, I'm not very effective physically. But I've got this white-haired guy behind me screaming "Go!"

We had a back-to-back series with Detroit, and in the first game, in their Joe Louis Arena, Bob Probert was running around all over the ice doing whatever he wanted. While we were on the airplane going back to Toronto, Brophy came up to my seat.

"I really don't like to tell players to do this," he said, "but you've gotta get Probert."

Two days before the game and he's telling me that! Of course, when the game arrived, Probert went out and started tossing the Leafs' star, Wendel Clark, around. So I'm sent on the ice to get after him. Probert and I were all lined up for the face-off and I really didn't know how to go about this. Hey, it wasn't difficult to get involved when somebody had done something to me first. What was I supposed to do here? I wasn't going to reach over and tap Probert on the shoulder, then say, "Excuse me, Bob, but I'm going to hit you now because that's what the guy behind our bench sent me out here to do." So I jumped him. I didn't do much besides get it over with as quickly as possible. My heart wasn't in this scrap, and I wasn't going to trust my fighting ability in a situation like that against a heavyweight who could throw them like Probert, simply because none of this was spontaneous. A very similar thing happened in St. Louis after Todd Ewing ran Borje Salming. I was right there and jumped on Ewing immediately. Now that was something I wouldn't normally have done, but I was thinking too much. I figured if I went back to that bench right away, Brophy would just send me right back out to get into something, and I'd probably get hurt because my heart wasn't in it.

The older I got, the more drastic something had to be to get a reaction from me. I had a hair-trigger temper when I was younger, but in that 1987-88 season, the last year of my career, it became more and more impossible to play the role Brophy wanted me to play. Luke Richardson was only an eighteen-year-old kid, Toronto's first-round draft choice, during the season I played for Toronto. And one night, against Edmonton, he met up with Kelly Buchberger, who's always eager to fight anybody. We're talking about a couple of young guys, both well over six feet tall and each weighing a couple of hundred pounds. And both willing to go. But Luke lost the fight and came away with his nose broken. We got it at the bench from Brophy and even more in the dressing room between periods. Hey, pardon me, but Richardson was a rookie. When I was a rookie, I'd have been chomping at the bit to get back at the guy who'd bopped me. When I was eighteen, I sure as hell wouldn't have expected some twenty-eight-year-old veteran who had ten years in the league to go out there and fight my battles. And, to his credit, Luke didn't want me to. He went back out and stood up for himself. Brophy thought he had me pegged, that all he had to do was snap his fingers and I'd turn into some animal.

I dressed all the time, but I'd only get on the ice once or twice a game. Usually I'd get a shift to start off the game, but every period I'd loosen the tension on my skate laces. In the first period I knew I was going to get that one shift, so I'd have my skates done up tight. Second period they'd be a little looser. Toward the end of the third period, my laces were so loose that I could almost shake the skates off my feet. I went through this every single night. It got to the point that I just watched the clock and wanted the game over with as quickly as possible. I'd sit there on the bench hoping nobody from the other team would stick any of our players.

At the end, I didn't even want to go to the rink in Toronto. Marvette only came to two games and only then because my mom and dad were in town, visiting for Christmas. Why should she have bothered going to those games? So she could watch me sit? She might as well have stayed home and watched the game on TV. That's what I wanted to do. Every time I left the house to go to Maple Leaf Gardens, I'd stare at the TV before I went out the door and think, I'd give anything to be able to stay right here.

We lived near the waterfront in a condominium complex not far from the Harbour Castle hotel. My sunroom windows provided a great view of the lake and an even better view of my neighbors. I could catch a bus to Union Station and hop on the subway from there to Maple Leaf Gardens and make the whole trip in less than fifteen minutes, so I didn't have to put up with the senseless parking hassle that so many have to deal with in downtown Toronto. I didn't even have to own a vehicle. It was convenient, but how much does any of that mean when you don't want to go to work in the first place?

I had a soulmate in Greg Terrion. We weren't linemates or anything. The closest thing I had to linemates, what with the ice time I was getting from Brophy, were the trainer and stickboy. Greg was a good friend. He was the type of guy who could really play, even when he'd only come off the bench once in a while. He's a great skater, so he had no problem with that. He played a little more than me, which still wasn't much. There were lots of nights when we just sat there on the bench the whole night. We didn't slide down the bench, the

In 1984 with two of my biggest fans, my sons Kelly *(left)* and Jason.

Some fans go to extremes to express their loyalty.

With Dave Hunter, one of my closest friends dating back to the old WHA days.

way all the other players would do, keeping all their lines together. Greg and I just stayed down at one end of the bench, opening and closing the gate.

I was embarrassed. Here I was on the most-televised hockey team in North America. I had a lot of friends watching. My kids were home in Brandon living with their mom and watching me on national TV. My parents were watching. Even though I'd been a fighter and done all that stuff, they'd seen me win Stanley Cups. I'd played with the best team in hockey and I'd contributed to that team. Especially in our first Stanley Cup, I'd contributed in every way.

Now I was with the Toronto Maple Leafs. I'd gone from at least semiregular status with the number-one team in hockey and all of a sudden I can't get more than one shift on a team that's in twenty-first place in the NHL. Something was drastically wrong.

In December of 1987 I'd called up Brophy before a practice and said, "I'm thinking of doing something here and maybe you can talk me out of it." He came right over to my apartment and we had a long discussion. I told him I couldn't do this anymore. It would have been one thing if I was playing, but just sitting there all the time was something I couldn't handle. I had all this idle time and all these thoughts would keep buzzing through my head. I'd lived real well but it hadn't all been roses. I'd sit on that Toronto bench, thinking about my two boys and how I didn't get to see them very much. I'd think about getting ripped off for all that money by Spencer. I'd think of how I missed the people back in Edmonton. I've got to play hockey, I told Brophy. I've got to keep busy so I'm not dwelling on those things all the time.

If he wanted me to be effective at all, then he was going to have to play me more. If I was going to be any kind of a force to be reckoned with out there, the way I knew I could be, then I had to play more so things could be allowed to happen spontaneously. And Brophy agreed. He said he could do something about my ice time or, more specifically, my lack of it. I really figured we'd solved the problem because he sounded so sincere. I found out at the next game it was all just talk. Nothing changed.

I took it as long as I could, then snapped. There were six games left in the schedule and we were in Vancouver. That's when I left and went home to Edmonton. I should have waited a day. It wouldn't have cost me as much as it did to fly home because the team was going from Vancouver to Calgary and I could have got a cheaper fare from there, but I'd have paid anything to get out.

The last straw started on the team flight to Vancouver. We were going out a day early, supposedly to get used to the time change. I was with a few veterans who got to sit up front in the business class section. The three of us each had a beer, then had wine with our dinners. We didn't think much about it, because on a previous commercial flight from Toronto to Edmonton, our assistant coach, Garry Lariviere, had told us a little beer and wine was okay as long as we didn't get carried away.

But this time, Brophy singled me out.

"What the f------ are the rules for drinking on the airplane?" he said to me.

I started to answer him. As soon as I got the words "Well, the last time we went out to Edmonton we were allowed to have—" Brophy cut me off.

"I don't give a f------ what Edmonton does!" Brophy yelled. "They win all the time. We lose all the time. Montreal wins all the time. We lose."

I did the slowest possible boil the rest of the day. I was shaking. That night in Vancouver I ran into Paul Lawless. We'd become good friends during our days with the Hartford Whalers, before he'd been traded to the Canucks. Paul and I went out for a real nice dinner at Hy's Mansion and were going back to the hotel when it hit me; I had to get out. It had all come to the point where enough was enough. I called Marvette in Toronto, got the number of our credit card, and booked myself the first available flight to Edmonton.

I went back to my room and told my roomie, Greg Terrion, "Tubby, I've had enough. I'm going and you can tell that son of a bitch Brophy whatever you want to tell him."

Sometime later, Greg told me he wanted to come with me. He was going through hell, too, but he had a wife and kids to support and was in no position to walk. I don't know what it was that Tubby told Brophy. But I do know that the next day, when the Toronto reporters who were with the Leafs found out I was missing, they realized Terrion was my roommate, so they all went flocking over to him at the rink. Greg knew they'd be coming. And he was ready for them. He had a big strip of hockey tape across his mouth. He wasn't saying anything to anybody.

I'd promised to leave some game tickets for a friend, so I left them in Paul Lawless's care. He wished me luck and suddenly I was all alone at the airport at six o'clock in the morning.

What a relief! To arrive in Edmonton, hop in a cab, and get into familiar territory. I was home. The first thing I did was grab a newspaper to see what was going on. The Oilers were on a road trip. But it said Kevin Lowe was hurt and had stayed home. The second thing I did was phone Kevin.

"I'm AWOL and I'm over at David's on Argyle," I told him. "Let's get together."

Believe me, we did. I spent four days in Edmonton before going back to Toronto. And I only went back to clean up some loose ends. I never had any intention of returning to the Maple Leafs. My leaving hadn't been some case of being out late after a few too many and not knowing what I was doing. When I left them in Vancouver, I'd known exactly what was going on and all the consequences. I'd had enough hockey. It wasn't there anymore. They could have suspended me or fined me or whatever. It would have been cheap at half the price.

The year had started with so much promise of fun, right from training camp. There are a number of stretching exercises and calisthenics various teams like to do before they put their equipment on and go out onto the ice. A lot of teams like to hire an aerobics instructor during training camp to lead the players through those preskate workouts. A bunch of the Maple Leafs were out after practice one day at a strip joint in Toronto. Wendel Clark, Al Secord, and I were sitting at a table by ourselves when one of the strippers came over and sat down with us. Suddenly the light went on. We had a stroke of genius. It was too much to resist! We offered her $100 to come out and lead the team in our aerobics exercises the next morning. Then we phoned the real instructor and told her practice had been canceled.

It was perfect. This girl showed up and looked entirely legitimate. She had one of those fancy aerobics outfits. She even brought along her own ghetto blaster. So we've got about thirty-five guys in this room she's leading in the exercises and only the three of us knew what was really going on. Soon as the music started, she had everybody going through these stretching drills. Then we did some running on the spot and some bends and some jumps. We'd all been through these workouts so many times that they'd become boring. You end up just going through the motions without noticing what's happening around you. But she sure made these guys take notice. Just when she had them convinced she was the genuine article, she started to take off her clothes. Rookies' jaws were dropping on the floor all over the place. They didn't know what the hell was going on. It was $100 well spent.

What with my abrupt departure from Vancouver and all, I hadn't really had a chance to say goodbye to a lot of great guys on that Maple Leafs club. When I went back to Toronto right at the end of the 1987-88 season to get my belongings in order and organize my permanent move home to Edmonton, I called up Tubby Terrion in the Leafs' dressing room and found out the guys were going to congregate at a lounge called P.M. Toronto's. They were all there when I arrived, and when I walked in, they all stood up and started cheering.

"Sammy, you escaped!" the boys yelled.

"There's not a team that can hold me!" I yelled back.

And that was my farewell to the National Hockey League. A standing ovation from the Toronto Maple Leafs.

16

Life Goes On

The first fight I ever had in pro hockey was with Cam Connor. To this day, he claims that I caused him to go bald. We got into a wrestling match during the first World Hockey Association game I ever played, in Houston against the Aeros. Cam wasn't wearing a helmet and he had a lot of hair at the time, so I grabbed some of it. While I was hanging on to his hair, he was pulling at my pants, trying to get me off balance and flip me. It was like a teeter-totter: Cam tugging my pants and me yanking his hair. The fight itself was no big deal. But sometime later, when the Oilers went into the NHL, Cam was traded to Edmonton. When he showed up, I noticed he was getting a little shy of hair up front. Wouldn't you know it, he gave me hell! He said I started the whole balding process. You should see him now. Hey, I sure didn't do that much damage. I'd have had to pull for days.

The last fight I ever had in pro hockey? That one was with myself, deciding whether or not to leave the Maple Leafs. I kicked that one around for about three months before I realized I didn't want any more to do with John Brophy and his hockey club.

When I think back to the last couple of years of my career, especially the last one, I'm sure everybody on the opposing teams could see that I didn't have that glare in my eyes anymore. When I'd been serious about fighting people, I

149

could look right through them. At the end of my career, they were probably looking at me, thinking I was Bambi.

You can't fake it. If you're upset and you want to intimidate somebody, you can do it. But when you start to think you might take the shot that knocks you out, you can't do it anymore. It's fire and desire and I'd lost a lot of both, particularly when the opposition was the Edmonton Oilers. I'd enjoyed going back to Edmonton to play when I was with Hartford. The Whalers coach, Jack Evans, was a real laid-back guy who'd never do anything real stupid like order me to fight. But it was another story going back there with the Leafs. Brophy wouldn't hesitate about sending me out there. It wouldn't have been beyond him to send me out there against Gretz. That's how bad Brophy was. It wouldn't have surprised me at all for him to give me a tap on the shoulder and say, "Go rough Gretzky up a bit and take him off his game."

When I was with either Hartford or Toronto, I played against Edmonton the way I used to do as an Oiler during training camp. I'd get in people's way but I wasn't going to hurt anybody. I'd been part of that organization and had spent nine years with some of those guys. How was I supposed to try to hurt Mess? Or Kevin? And if anybody was ever stupid enough to think I was going to try to hurt Gretz, they should have been locked up. Can you imagine the trouble I'd have finding a place to hide today if I'd done something stupid like grab Wayne and pound a big hurt on him? One punch or big hit and it would have been all over for me. Everybody in Edmonton would have reverted to what they'd thought about me when I first started playing there.

I was booed enough back then. I had enough people thinking I was an overgrown goof. For years I tried my very best to change people's opinions. I tried to show them that I am a human being. I can talk. I can even read and write. But one incident like something Brophy would have been glad to create, had I been idiotic enough to go through with it, and I'd have been right back at square one. No, come to think about it, it probably would have set me back even further than that. They'd have watched me hit Gretz then said, "How about that. He is a goon, after all. He's programmed to do whatever he's told to do." Everything that I'd tried to build up over the years in Edmonton, everything I'd done to try to show these people that I wasn't the type of person they thought I was, would have been destroyed in one second.

Once I'd made my decision to retire, there was no going back. It was time for me to get out. I'd moved twice and dragged Marvette all over the country. She'd had to sell her business and get something else going. Then she'd had to forget that, just to follow me. It was unfair to her to move again. She was going to start working in Edmonton. I wanted to live there. So what was the point of packing up, going to another city, finding another place on a short-term lease, plus maintaining our own home in Edmonton. You never know what sort of situation you can get into. I could just as easily have wound up on the bench somewhere else. Nothing's for sure in hockey. The only pro hockey alternative other than the NHL was Europe. And there wasn't a helluva lot of sense in me going there. Not with their rules. Can you imagine me playing in Switzerland? One frown and I'd have been deported.

As for management, no thank you. When Guy Lafleur and Jacques Lemaire played for the Canadiens, they were more than teammates in Montreal. In their greatest years, they were linemates. All of a sudden, Lemaire's the coach of the Canadiens and he's benching his friend Lafleur. I couldn't do it. First of all, I could never enforce curfews. That would have been a real laugh. For them, that is. They'd all know they could stay out real late and still beat me home. Attitudes have to change when you move to the coaching side. But I couldn't have made that change. I'd know toward the end of each practice that the guys were chomping at the bit to get out of there and go for a cold beer. And I'd know I couldn't go with them. I couldn't be part of that group without all those players wondering if I was some sort of spy for management.

So it was time to say goodbye to hockey and stay in Edmonton where I could get on with the rest of my life. It was time for a fresh start. There was no sense trying to hang on to something that wasn't there for me anymore. I hate the thought of a player hanging on, of being traded from team to team for no other reason than to collect a paycheck, no matter what size the check happens to be. The game's got to be enjoyable.

I'd been a lucky man during my career. In eleven years, the most serious injury I'd ever suffered was a bunged-up knee that kept me on the sidelines for seven weeks. And even that wasn't all bad. Dave Lumley was hurt at the time, too, so I had some great company in the therapy room. Back then, being injured wasn't the end of the world. You'd just ice your knee or ride the bike. There was nobody around to bother you. You were on your honor. At least, you were supposed to be. Mostly, Lummer and I were on our bar stools. That's all changed drastically. They have a full-time therapist now. Toward the end of my career, while I was still with the Oilers, I hurt my back and had to meet the therapist in his clinic every morning at seven o'clock. Then, at noon, I had to show up at the University of Alberta for more therapy. There was all that and skating drills, too. I'm telling you, it's no fun to be injured anymore.

Once I'd been traded, I went through the motions. I wasn't happy being in Hartford. I thought it was sort of a cruel joke, that Slats was trying to get me back for all the curfews I'd missed over the years. I dreamed and hoped the whole reason Hartford had acquired me was to fill in for their tough guy, Torrie Robertson, who'd broken his leg. I thought — hoped — I was there on a temporary basis to fill in as the DH and when Robertson got healthy again, they'd swing another deal to send me back to Edmonton. That's the way I wanted it, but that isn't the way it worked out. There was nothing wrong with Hartford, but the city didn't seem like a hockey town. I felt like I was in the minors, where the people's attitude was Hockey? Ho hum, so what? That didn't totally surprise me. But Toronto sure did, especially inside that Maple Leaf dressing room.

We'd had a lot of pride in our uniforms in Edmonton. You didn't casually throw your sweater at the trainer or at the laundry bin after a game. You might miss and your sweater could land on the floor. And that was a cardinal sin. It was a mark of disrespect to your team. I was shocked that nobody ever seemed to worry about that stuff in Toronto. That sweater and its Maple Leaf crest are world famous. They've been around for years and years. But I've watched Toronto players casually flip their jerseys toward the table after a game, have it miss, and land on the floor, then just let it lie there. I'd be the first one to go and grab it and put it back up on that table. I never made a big speech or a big fuss about it, but it really upset me a lot. I'd just put the sweater back and hope somebody else said something. But nobody ever did. It bugged me, even though I was with Toronto for such a short time and I was hardly proud to be a Maple Leaf doing the things that Brophy wanted me to do.

In Edmonton, if somebody flipped a sweater toward the bin where we'd put them after each game and it missed, you wouldn't believe how many guys would rush over to pick it up. They'd take that person aside and tell him how very lucky he was to be part of the team, how happy he should be to be one of only 400 people who were allowed to play in this league and that there were guys who'd do almost anything to be a member of a Stanley Cup champion team.

That's Edmonton, a franchise that really hasn't been around very long. But in Toronto, which next to Montreal is supposed to be Canada's hotbed of hockey with all that tradition, sweaters were lying around all over the floor. It doesn't matter if you're the champ or you're in the middle of losing fifteen in a row. You've got to have pride in what you wear and what that represents.

You also need common sense. I'm not the greatest living example of that in the whole wide world and don't pretend to be. But if I was ever to offer any advice to youngsters coming into the NHL, it would be to put themselves on a budget right from the word go and stick to it like Krazy Glue. Get everything you need to live on — money set aside for clothes, rent and necessities — then tuck away whatever you can. When you come out of junior and suddenly you're making something in the neighborhood of a six-figure salary, the money seems like it comes from some bottomless pit that'll never run out. Well, it does. It's easy to blow. Trust me. I know that for sure.

You've got to get a good accountant or a good financial

adviser, or both, to help you along because you're just not going to be ready to handle all this on your own. What it comes down to in the end is finding somebody you can trust. Don't be afraid to talk. Talk to as many people as you want to until you find the person you're prepared to trust. Look for an established person in an established firm. The last thing you need is some fly-by-night guy. There are a lot of them out there, believe me.

There's a great move on now that'd really help a lot of kids and that's for bonded agents. There's a whole list of guys like that available who've been investigated by the NHL. It's still up to the individual. You can talk to whoever you want to. But if you stick with these approved, bonded people, then if something goes wrong, you're not going to get screwed out of your money.

It's important that young players get someone to help set them up on a budget. Then you can tuck the money away and, believe me, you don't have all that long to do the tucking. I played eleven years of pro hockey. They seem to have flown by like a month, and the money was gone before I knew it.

I made some real decent money over the years. If I hadn't run into that agent and had planned for the future the way I should have, it would have been a different story for me right now. There'd have been no immediate panic to get out and find a job as soon as I left hockey. But you need someone to help with investments. I didn't know anything about money at all. I mean nothing whatsoever. I thought blue-chip stocks were blue. I had no idea what a portfolio was and how to handle it.

You've also got to realize that playing hockey isn't going to be all games. Anybody who goes into it thinking it's all one big laugh is in for an enormous shock. For one thing, just getting to the arena for the games can be a nightmare at times, which is something anybody who's ever played for an NHL franchise in the western part of Canada or the United States can tell you all about. It's amazing how easy the travel is when you play in the East. It's a joke. I found that out when I was with Hartford and Toronto. Playing in Edmonton, we just didn't know any better. So we had to change planes at three airports to get to Washington. No big deal. We just did it. Didn't everybody? Then when you get to play for a team based down East, you discover how nice it is to charter into some city and charter right back to your own home and your own bed that night.

When I was younger, I couldn't wait to get out of town and kick up my heels. After a while, I discovered it wasn't quite as glamorous as a lot of people, including me, thought it would be to be on the road all the time. On my very first road trip in the pros, from Edmonton to Houston, we had a stopover in Las Vegas. As I was to learn real quickly, that was a pure fluke. We weren't jet-setters in the NHL. Not by a long shot. And it wasn't much fun being on the road, living out of your suitcase for a couple of weeks. The routine was so boring: go to the airport, fly somewhere, change planes and hope you can find space in the overhead bin, land, clear customs, hop on a bus, go to the hotel, have supper, sleep, get on the bus and go to the rink in the morning for a skate, then hop back on the bus to return to the hotel for a pregame meal and a sleep, then hop on the bus, return to the rink, play the game, then bus to the airport and fly somewhere else. It's all buses, hotels, airplanes, and terminals. It can wear you down a lot more than the hockey does.

Then there's the pressure to perform. It might not be true to say that you're only as good as your last game. But you sure as hell don't want to have too many bad ones in a row if you intend to make a dollar in the NHL. A lot of people look at hockey players and figure they've got it all aced. They make six figures a year. The hotels and flights are paid for. They get a healthy daily living allowance on the road. I'm not going to try to tell you that pro athletes don't have a pretty good thing going for themselves. But they do whatever it is they do for a short period of time, and I'm really not sure if people appreciate how much pressure is involved.

I was so fortunate. I never worried about getting traded when I was with Edmonton, and I was lucky enough to stay with them for nine years. A lot of guys only last three or four years and they've got trade rumors hanging over their heads all that time. That can make it pretty tough to sleep at night, especially for the married guys with a couple of kids at home to worry about. When I was traded from Edmonton to Hartford, then from Hartford to Toronto, I didn't have to worry about moving a family. It was easy for me. It's always easier for the player. He's going to a new team and immediately inherits twenty to twenty-five new friends. But players' wives or girlfriends have a tougher adjustment, particularly if there are kids involved who have to leave their friends at a very young age, pull up stakes, and start at a brand-new school with an entirely different group of children. Then five months later, they could all be looking at another move. That's the real down side of sports in a game where the average career is three or four years long. I got into the pros when I was twenty and played until I was thirty-one. And I'm planning to live for a lot of years yet. So really, whenever I did think of those eleven years in hockey and even though I might have thought it would never end, hockey's such a small piece of my life.

When you play, you've got to find that strength and motivation to win because that's what the whole thing is all about. Nobody's paying you to finish second. When I look back on it, that's probably what those pictures on the Oilers' "Wall of Fame" that we lugged around during the playoffs every year were all about. Were they part of what's called "sports psychology"? Probably. Psychology's a wonderful thing, if you want it. Just as long as you don't try to cram it down someone else's throat when he isn't interested. There are a lot of people willing to pay good money to listen to sports psychologists. Fine. If you're really interested, it can be worthwhile. But when it's four in the afternoon and you've gone through two sessions on the ice that day, then all of a sudden you're told to go listen to a lecture, imagine how short your attention span can be.

It's amazing how willing you can be to listen when you really want to learn, though. When I was just starting into my prelicensing real estate course, they gave me this huge textbook. I opened it up, took one look at all this technical stuff, and figured, scratch this garbage. I don't want to be a bloody lawyer. I just want to be a realtor.

But I went to every hour of those classes, and strange as it might sound, at the end of it I wanted more. Sitting in a classroom going through a book just isn't me. At least it never had been before. In school, if they told us we'd have a test coming up next month, I'd immediately know I was going to be sick that day. Craving knowledge was totally out of character for me. But here I was at the end of this real estate course, feeling that I wouldn't mind all the extra days they'd like to offer me. I didn't just want to pass the examination, I wanted to do really well. If they'd doubled the price for just one more day, I'd have been glad to pay it.

That's going to be my life from now on. And whatever success I might have at it, I know I'm going to owe a lot of it to hockey, particularly to those fabulous years with the Edmonton Oilers, to the great guys I played with, and the fame that came with being associated with those Stanley Cup champions.

I'm playing a little Old Timers' hockey now. The team I'm on has a starting line of Dave "Tiger" Williams, Dave "The Hammer" Schultz, and me. Imagine, me, the choirboy of my line!

I'm getting better all the time, though. I was the twenty-fifth pick in the draft when Minnesota chose me back in 1977. Now the NHL's talking expansion again. I sure hope so. I keep hoping the league will expand to twenty-five teams. Then I'll be able to say I was a first-round draft choice.

The game! Oh, it'll change. But not all that much. Not at the NHL level. I was reading just a while ago that Wayne Gretzky says they've got to take fighting out of hockey.

I can understand that. I've seen Gretz fight.